BLESSED REASSURANCE

Finding Security in Christ

By
John B. Woodward, D.Min.

BLESSED REASSURANCE
© 2008 by John B. Woodward

Published by
Grace Fellowship International
P. O. Box 368
Pigeon Forge, TN 37868   USA

GraceFellowshipIntl.com
GraceNotebook.com
BiblicalPsychology.com
Phone: (865) 429-0450
john@gracenotebook.com

ISBN 978-0-9724343-2-4

Cover Design and Photography by Mark S. Phillips
www.marksphillips.com

Printed by
Lightning Source Inc.
1246 Heil Quaker Blvd.
La Vergne, TN 37086 USA
www.lightningsource.com

Scripture quotations (unless indicated otherwise) are from
The Holy Bible, New King James Version
© 1982 by Thomas Nelson, Inc.

Library of Congress Cataloging-in-Publication Data

Woodward, John B. (John Bradford), 1955-
   Blessed Reassurance: Finding Security in Christ/by John B. Woodward.
      p. cm.
   Includes bibliographical references and index.
   ISBN 0-9724343-2-1 (pbk. : alk. paper)
   1. Assurance (Theology) I. Title.
   BT785.W66 2008
   234--dc22
                                    2008037473

Dedication

This book has been prepared to encourage believers who have lacked the personal assurance of their salvation and security in Christ.

From 1982 through 1989 my wife, Linda, and I were blessed to serve with the Peoples Church of Montreal. I was enriched by the mentoring of Pastor Frank Humphrey, Ph.D. and the loving fellowship with the international congregation of this vital, urban church.

I dedicate *Blessed Reassurance* to the ministry of Peoples Church.

To God be the glory.

John B. Woodward

Acknowledgements

I would like to express my appreciation to the staff and constituency of Grace Fellowship International for their encouragement to complete and publish this book. I thank Cathy Solomon for doing the layout and adding corrections from my proof readers including Geri Dilbeck, J. B. Woodward, Sr., and Charles Solomon.

The covered bridge theme on the book's cover was selected to symbolize the bridge of salvation as sheltered by God's grace and faithfulness. I thank Mark Phillips for his photograph of the bridge in Milton, West Virginia; it was originally constructed in 1876. My interest in covered bridges goes back to my courtship with Linda. We used to drive around Pennsylvania locating them. When I proposed marriage to her on March 5, 1977, we were at Van Sandt's bridge in Bucks county. Thankfully, she said "yes."

Lastly, I thank friends who designated contributions to enable the publication of *Blessed Reassurance.*

Table of Contents

PART 1   STUDIES ON ASSURANCE

PART 2   STUDIES ON REASSURANCE

APPENDICES

Foreword

The assurance of eternal life through Jesus Christ our Lord and Savior is an amazing truth. An aspect of this assurance is the doctrine of eternal security. It is a teaching that has often been criticized for justifying an irresponsible and substandard approach to the Christian life. This criticism, though often well intended, misses the mark. The eternal security of the believer is a clear reminder that our salvation draws its source not from us but from Him who loved us and gave Himself up for our transgressions! As such, God gives us the motivation to live for Him since we know as David told Goliath "the battle is the LORD's!" "Thanks be to God who gives us the victory through our Lord Jesus Christ!"

Dr. John Woodward has presented an excellent exposition of this teaching that will serve to encourage Christians to see the wonder of their position in Christ. He carefully deals with the problems of "false assurance," and shows the biblical evidence for "true assurance." He deals with a variety of biblical texts including those often cited in challenging this understanding. He does it with grace and a careful reading of the texts in question. I appreciate the overall presentation he has given in this book.

On a personal note, it was a delight to minister with John for seven and a half years at Peoples Church of Montreal during the 1980's. It has always been a pleasure to have him in our pulpit when he is in town.

This book will serve an important role in the lives of many Christians and I commend it to you for your growth in grace.

To God be the glory!

Rev. Francis Humphrey, Ph.D.
Senior Pastor
Peoples Church of Montreal

Preface

One of the issues that frequently comes up in Christian discipleship and counseling is the need for personal assurance and security in the spiritual life. Chronic doubt and uncertainty are like pebbles in your shoe; they make your Christian walk painful and unsteady. These struggles with insecurity are by no means limited to those who are young in the faith.

Evangelist D. L. Moody referred to the importance of assurance in the lives of Christian leaders:

> After John Wesley had been preaching for some time, someone said to him, "Are you sure, Mr. Wesley, of your salvation?" "Well," he answered, "Jesus Christ died for the whole world." "Yes, we all believe that; but are you sure that you are saved?" Wesley replied that he was sure that provision had been made for his salvation. "But are you sure, Wesley, that you are saved?" It went like an arrow to his heart, and he had no rest or power until that question was settled.

> Many men and many women go on month after month, and year after year, without power, because they do not know their standing in Christ; they are not sure of their own footing for eternity. [Hugh] Latimer wrote [Nicholas] Ridley once that when he was settled and steadfast about his own salvation he was as bold as a lion, but if that hope became eclipsed he was fearful and afraid and was disqualified for service. Many are disqualified for service because they are continually doubting their own salvation.[1]

I have had the same experience. After being saved at a young age and growing up in church, I had gnawing doubts about my relationship with God. It wasn't until I went off to Bible college and began studying God's Word personally, that I found answers to my questions and gained a firm assurance.

We shouldn't need to enroll in college courses to settle the issue of security in Christ. The following chapters cover a variety of topics and texts that relate to gaining and retaining confidence in the believer's relationship with God. [This volume does not claim to exhaustively cover every facet of assurance. Yet if some of my fellow followers of Christ discover confidence and clarity through these pages, the book will have served its purpose.]

In part one, *Studies on Assurance*, we will seek to clarify the difference between false assurance (thinking one is saved, when in reality he/she is not) and true salvation (being saved and enjoying the confidence that this salvation has been fully accomplished). These chapters will support assurance based on the nature of God's redemption, and themes that support this saving grace.

In part two, *Studies on Reassurance*, the chapters explore objections and challenges to the doctrine of a secure salvation. Popular issues and challenging passages will be explored to defend the promises of God's faithfulness to keep His children secure in His love and grace.

[1] D.L. Moody, *Moody's Anecdotes*, 101-102.

Note: Some biblical quotations contain italicized words. In the New King James Version, editors use italics for implied words (not in the original Hebrew or Greek manuscripts). However, in this book, italics in Bible passages are editorial choices of this author. They indicate "emphasis added."

When a reference is given after a biblical quotation, it refers to its location. Additional references (or references that are not direct biblical quotations) are included as supporting and relevant verses. Due to the book's numerous cross references, the usual "cf." [Latin—confer, meaning "compare"] will not be used before each cross reference.

Blessed Reassurance

PART 1

Studies on Assurance

Blessed Reassurance

Chapter 1
How to Gain True Assurance

When I embarked as a high school graduate from Atlanta, Georgia to Florida Bible College, one of my main concerns was to gain the assurance of my salvation. On my parents' recommendation and sponsorship, I planned to get a year of biblical training as a foundation for my future career, whatever that might be. Although I received Christ as my personal Savior at an early age and attended church with my family, I read only little of the Bible. In my middle teen years I lacked a deeper commitment to eternal values.

So off to Bible college I went. The school's enthusiastic student body, the consistent Christian fellowship, and the effective Bible teaching made a lasting impact on my life. It wasn't too long before I reaffirmed my faith in Christ's finished work on the Cross and my allegiance to Him as my Lord. The promises of God's Word made it clear that I had a solid basis for the assurance of my salvation. Thankfully, this blessed security has supported my growth in grace ever since.

I am often asked if the Bible teaches "once saved, always saved." And, related questions: Can the child of God lose his or her salvation? What about those who are *backslidden*? Does belief in the eternal security of the born-again Christian tempt a believer to live as he/she pleases? Let's seek a balanced, biblical answer to these questions.

Consider the Danger of False Assurance

Before exploring the Scriptures about security, we acknowledge that many people who think that they are Christians are not truly saved. This conclusion is based on Christ's warning in the Sermon on the Mount:

> Enter by the narrow gate; for wide is the gate and broad is the way that leads to destruction, and there are many who go in by it. Because narrow is the gate and difficult is the way which leads to life, and there are few who find it...Many will say to Me in that day, "Lord, Lord, have we not prophesied in Your name, cast out demons in Your name, and done many wonders in Your name?" And then I will declare to them, "I never knew you; depart from Me, you who practice lawlessness!" (Matt. 7:13,14,22,23).

It would be tragic to have false assurance and no salvation!

What is the difference between merely professing faith and really possessing faith? Saving faith opens the heart's door to the indwelling of God's Holy Spirit (Rom. 8:9; John 1:12). The Holy Spirit's presence will be seen in the believer's good works and continued faith (James 2:14-19; Col. 3:23). Children of God have His love for their brothers and sisters in Christ (1 John 4:7-16).[1]

In the Great Commission, Christ commanded that all of His disciples be *baptized* in water as an outward testimony of their conversion. But, going forward at a meeting, praying a sinner's prayer, even being water baptized, does not prove someone is converted to Christ. Repentance is the "flip side of the coin" of saving faith in Christ (Acts 17:30). It involves conviction of our guilt before a holy God, our inability to save ourselves, and a cry for mercy to escape hell. There is a cost to following Christ, but it costs more not to follow Him! (Luke 9:23,57-62).

Some identify themselves as Christians, but their departure from the faith reveals that they never were born again. As the apostle John put it,

> They went out from us, but they were not of us; for if they had been of us, they would have continued with us; but they went out that they might be made manifest, that none of them were of us (1 John 2:19; John 3:3).

Let's not miss this: *good works are the fruit of salvation, not the root.* We are not saved by a mixture of faith and works of merit; we are saved by grace through faith plus zero! "But to him who does not work but believes on Him who justifies the ungodly, his faith is accounted for righteousness" (Rom. 4:5; Eph. 2:8,9). We are fully to depend upon Christ for salvation, not ourselves or a church. In light of this, the apostle Paul exhorts us:

> Examine yourselves to see whether you are in the faith; test yourselves. Do you not realize yourselves, that Christ Jesus is in you?—unless, of course, you fail the test?" (2 Cor. 13:4,5 NIV; 2 Pet. 1:10).

Instead of telling a professing Christian "You are saved!," you could say, "If you have true faith in the true Jesus, God's Word assures you of salvation" (John 5:24; Gal. 1:8). Now, let's study the scriptural basis for true assurance.

First, consider the *objective testimony* for assurance of the believer's salvation. This relates to the reality of our right standing with God—whether or not we personally *feel* saved or mentally grasp our security in Christ.

We are told that God's promises are exceedingly great and precious (2 Pet. 1:4) and they equip us for Christian living (2 Pet. 1:3). Here are some promises for you if you are in Christ:

1. Salvation is given to you in this life, not just on Judgment Day:

    "Most assuredly, I say to you, he who hears My word and believes in Him who sent Me *has* everlasting life, and shall not come into judgment, but *has passed* [past tense] from death into life" (John 5:24).

2. Christ will never lose you:

    "My sheep hear My voice, and I know them, and they follow Me. And I give them eternal life, and *they shall never perish*; neither shall anyone snatch them out of My hand. My Father, who has given them to Me, is greater than all; and no one is able to snatch them out of My Father's hand" (John 10:27-29).

3. Jesus will never cast you out or lose you:

    "All that the Father gives Me will come to Me, and the one who comes to Me *I will by no means cast out.* This is the will of the Father who sent Me, that of all He has given Me I should lose nothing, but should raise it up at the last day" (John 6:37,39).

4. Eternal life is your present possession:

    "Most assuredly, I say to you, he who believes in Me *has* [present tense] ever-lasting life" (John 6:47).

5. God is faithful to keep you:

    "... for I know whom I have believed and am persuaded that *He is able to keep* what I have committed to Him until that Day" (2 Tim. 1:12).

6. You are spiritually united with Christ Himself:

    "If [since] then you were raised with Christ, seek those things which are above, where Christ is, sitting at the right hand of God. For you died, and *your life is hidden with Christ in God.* When Christ who is our life appears, then you also will appear with Him in glory" (Col 3:1,3,4).

7. You can know that you have eternal life:

    "These things I have written to you who believe in the name of the Son of God, that you may know that you have eternal life, and that you may continue to believe in the name of the Son of God" (1 John 5:13).

Finding security in Christ requires you to claim God's promises by faith.

This episode in Wilbur Chapman's life demonstrates the importance of objective assurance:

When Dr. J. Wilbur Chapman was a student for the ministry...he heard the famous evangelist D. L. Moody speak. Charmed by Moody's simple presentation, Chapman followed him from one service to another. Finally he told Moody that he didn't have the assurance of salvation. Though he was studying for the ministry, one day he was sure that he would be in heaven, then the next day was in despair for he did not know for sure if he were saved. Moody pointed to the verse, "Truly, truly, I say to you, he who hears My word and believes in Him who sent Me has everlasting life, and shall not come into condemnation, but has passed from death into life" [John 5:24].

Moody asked, "Do you believe on the Son?" "Yes," replied the young student. "Will you come into condemnation?" "That's just what I don't know for sure. That's why I came to see you" answered the young man. Then D. L. Moody said in his firm way of dealing with people, "See here, young man, whom are you doubting?" In a flash it dawned on young Chapman that he was doubting none other than the Lord Jesus Christ, whose word is truth and cannot be broken. That was the beginning of better days for young Chapman. He never doubted his salvation from that day on, and became an evangelist known the world over.[2]

Objective assurance is nothing less than taking God at his word: "In hope [anticipation with joy] of eternal life which God, who cannot lie, promised before time began" (Titus 1:2; 1 John 5:9). As the hymn declares,

Standing on the promises of Christ my King,
Through eternal ages let His praises ring;
Glory in the highest I will shout and sing,
Standing on the promises of God.

Standing on the promises that cannot fail,
When the howling storms of doubt and fear assail;
By the living Word of God I shall prevail,
Standing on the promises of God.

Standing on the promises of Christ the Lord,
Bound to Him eternally by love's strong chord;

Overcoming daily with the Spirit's sword.
Standing on the promises of God.

Standing on the promises I cannot fall,
List'ning every moment to the Spirit's call;
Resting in my Savior as my all in all,
Standing on the promises of God.[3]

So, fellow believer be encouraged that God will never cast you out or lose you. He is the ultimate promise keeper!

[1] For the importance of the "tests" of true Christians in the epistle of 1 John, see Phil Jones *How to Exchange Your Life for a New One* (Pigeon Forge, TN: Grace Fellowship Publishing), 2002, 1-4.

[2] Leslie Flynn, *Come Alive with Illustrations*, (Grand Rapids: Baker), 115.

[3] Text and music by R. Kelso Carter, *Standing on the Promises.*

Chapter 2
How to Gain True Assurance
(Continued)

In each issue of Readers' Digest magazine, there is a feature article identified as Drama in Real Life. The stories are exciting adventures of near-death mishaps and heroic rescues. What a relief to follow the narrative to the point where those in danger are delivered.

This reminds me of an illustration used by one of my teachers. He clarified the nature of assured salvation this way.

> Imagine that you were drowning in the ocean and a rescue boat arrived just in time. If the sailor threw you a *How to Swim* book, would you be saved? No! Even so, we need more than an instructor, we need a *savior!* If the sailor dove into the water and swam around you, demonstrating the way to swim, would that save you? No! Even so, we need more than example, we need a *savior!* And what if the sailor pulled you into the boat, dried you off, took you within a few miles of the shore and threw you back in?! Would that save you? No! You would only be saved if you were pulled into the rescue boat and brought all the way to shore.

Even so, real salvation is a secure salvation.

The Lord Jesus is our instructor and our perfect example, but most important, He is the Savior and Keeper of all who come to Him in sincere repentance and faith. The writer of Hebrews summarizes our objective assurance: "Therefore He is also able to save to the uttermost those who come to God through Him, since He always lives to make intercession for them" (Heb. 7:25).

In part two of this study on assurance, we continue with *the subjective aspect* of our assurance in Christ. This relates to our awareness that we really are saved and kept by God. Although many people in Christendom are not really saved (Matt. 7:21-23), many are truly saved yet have doubts about their salvation. Perhaps you are one of them!

The apostle Paul encourages us with the promise that the Holy Spirit gives an internal "amen" to the child of God: "...You received the Spirit of adoption by whom we cry out, 'Abba, Father.' The Spirit Himself bears witness with our spirit that we are children of God" (Rom. 8:15,16). When we are focused on worship, the Lord can give us an inner assurance of our relationship with Him.

The presence of God's Spirit in the believer's life is a powerful testimony of security. As the book of Ephesians puts it,

> In Him [Christ] you also trusted, after you heard the word of truth, the gospel of your salvation; in whom also, having believed, you were sealed with the Holy Spirit of promise, who is *the guarantee* of our inheritance [heaven] until the redemption of the purchased possession [the believer's resurrection body], to the praise of His glory" (Eph. 1:12-14; Rom. 8:23).

In Bible times, a seal was a mark of ownership, a symbol of security, and a proof of authenticity. The Spirit of God is all this to God's people! So, we are urged to "not grieve the Holy Spirit of God, by whom you were *sealed* for the day of redemption" (Eph. 4:30). The Day of Redemption is the final installment of our conformity to the image of Christ. We will be like Him physically at the future Resurrection Day! (Phil. 3:20,21; Rom. 8:29).

As we abide in Christ, the evidence of our new life in Him becomes evident to ourselves and to others. We are recognized as the people of God by our good fruit (Matt. 7:20). The inner spiritual witness and the outer character witness contribute to the *subjective awareness* of our assured salvation.

The story is told of a newcomer to Alaska who started to cross a frozen river. As he walked along, he thought he heard a cracking sound and became frightened that the ice might break under him. He carefully lowered himself to distribute his weight more fully across the ice in hopes that it wouldn't give way. After twenty minutes of cautious crawling, he heard the sound of a Jeep starting up on the other side of the frozen river. A few minutes later the Jeep sped past him to the other shore! With renewed confidence, the timid traveler got up and walked the rest of the river's span with great relief. Note this: although the traveler had an *objective* basis of assurance (thick ice), he did not have *subjective* assurance until the Jeep drove across the frozen river, demonstrating the ice's strength.

How about you? Do you need to refocus your faith on the objective evidence of God's salvation promises? Or perhaps you need to strengthen the subjective enjoyment of this assurance by becoming sensitive to the spiritual witness of the indwelling Holy Spirit.

Now we need to compare the believer's *position* and *condition*. The former is objective; the latter is subjective

What is our position in Christ? The Bible declares: "There is therefore now no condemnation to those who are in Christ Jesus" (Rom. 8:1). We stand in grace, not our own merit: "Therefore, having been justified by faith, we have peace with God through our Lord Jesus Christ, through whom also we have access by faith into this *grace* in which we stand, and rejoice in hope of the glory of God" (Rom 5:1,2). Our position in Christ does not fluctuate.

Then, what is our personal condition? This depends on our daily walk. Will we reckon ourselves dead to the authority of sin and alive to the righteousness of God? (Rom. 6:5-11; 1 John 1:7-9; Eph. 5:18). As our response varies, so our condition fluctuates.

Now we come to a much-debated issue: Does assurance reduce the believer's incentive for godly living? Security in Christ—rightly understood—draws us closer to Him. "We love Him because He first loved us" (1 John 4:19). The goodness of God leads us to repentance (Rom. 2:4) and the grace of God teaches us to say "no" to ungodliness (Titus 2:11,12). As members of God's family, we are disciplined by Him if we go astray (Heb. 12:6; 1 Cor. 11:29-32). The future Judgment Seat of Christ will reveal how we responded to the opportunities of our earthly pilgrimage. This evaluation will determine our rewards or lack of them (2 Cor. 5:10; 1 Cor. 3:11-15). So, the quality of our Christian walk is very important.

True assurance inspires the Christian to a more devoted life of discipleship. Miles Stanford wrote:

> The believer who truly stands in the grace of positional security is the one who most fully fears God and hates sin. And he hates sin for what it is, not just for its consequences. Moreover, his is not a slavish fear; it is not the fear of losing God's love, but of offending and grieving it...The truth of security holds the Christian firm in the midst of the process of growth. It is the insecure believer who is naturally unstable and flounders from one "experience" to another, never learning and therefore never arriving at the truth. Resting in our eternal position frees us from the futile and sinful self-effort of trying to make our condition the basis of our security. Abiding in our eternal security in Christ gives the steadi-

ness of faith necessary for the ministry of the Holy Spirit to carry on His gracious ministry within—that of dealing with self in crucifixion, and thereby causing us to "grow in the grace and knowledge of our Lord and Savior Jesus Christ" (2 Pet. 3:18).[2]

The secure believer is also more equipped to stand against the devil—"the accuser of the brethren" (Rev. 12:10). The disciple is assured of protection by the spiritual armor of God. The belt of truth, the breastplate of righteousness, the shoes of the gospel of peace, the helmet of salvation, the shield of faith, and the sword of the Spirit are all fortifications of spiritual security. Armed with such true assurance we can stand firm! (Eph. 6:10-17).

The practical value of assurance was illustrated during the construction of the Golden Gate Bridge in California. At the time it was to be the longest, highest, most expensive bridge in the world. Because of the dangerous conditions, however, construction proceeded slowly; and the crew fell behind schedule. Someone figured out that insecurity hindered the workmen from concentration on their jobs. To remedy the situation, a giant safety net was suspended underneath the construction area. This innovative measure cost about a hundred thousand dollars. Yet because the risk of death was removed, the workman could focus on the project; and the construction advanced at a much faster rate.[3]

Similarly, true assurance supports the believer's walk with God. We live as those "accepted in the Beloved" [Christ—Eph 1:6]. Paul affirmed that God's grace and love inspires our confidence in Him. Savor this confidence-building Scripture passage:

He who did not spare His own Son, but delivered Him up for us all, how shall He not with Him also freely give us all things? Who shall bring a charge against

God's elect? It is God who justifies. Who is he who condemns? It is Christ who died, and furthermore is also risen, who is even at the right hand of God, who also makes intercession for us. Who shall separate us from the love of Christ? Shall tribulation, or distress, or persecution, or famine, or nakedness, or peril, or sword? As it is written: "For Your sake we are killed all day long; We are accounted as sheep for the slaughter." Yet in all these things we are more than conquerors through Him who loved us. For I am persuaded that neither death nor life, nor angels nor principalities nor powers, nor things present nor things to come, nor height nor depth, nor any other created thing, shall be able to separate us from the love of God which is in Christ Jesus our Lord (Rom. 8:32-39).

What a wonderful Savior and Keeper! Abide in the One who gives you true assurance.

[1] See GraceNote: *Motivations for Choosing God's Best.*

[2] Miles J. Stanford, *The Complete Green Letters* (Zondervan), 97.

[3] Leslie B. Flynn, *Come Alive with Illustrations*, 115.

Blessed Reassurance

Chapter 3
Soul Rest

In Tennessee, I visited friends who live in a log house over-looking the Smoky Mountains. Behind their house, amidst the trees, is a hammock. They described how good it feels to come home after a day's work, climb into that hammock, and relax in its swaying embrace.

What a picture of rest. We need times of rest for our bodies, but we also long for a rest for our *souls*. Like the Galatian Christians, many have "begun in the Spirit" (have been saved by grace), but are trying to be "made perfect by the flesh" (Gal. 3:1-3). The result is that we serve God with self-effort and end up exhausted.

Martha lapsed into this common, however well-intentioned, syndrome. You recall that Jesus and his disciples were staying with His friends, Martha, Mary, and Lazarus:

> Martha was distracted with much serving, and she approached Him and said, "Lord, do You not care that my sister has left me to serve alone? Therefore tell her to help me." And Jesus answered and said to her, "Martha, Martha, you are worried and troubled about many things. But one thing is needed, and Mary has chosen that good part, which will not be taken away from her" (Luke 10:40-42).

Of course, some time for preparing food was needed (this was before the days of take-out pizza). Yet, even when duty calls, grace can provide an inner rest. This perspective requires personal, focused time with the Lord like Mary appreciated. We can rely on His strength to serve with a heart of joy, since we are already accepted by God through grace (Rom. 5:1,2).

We are to rest in Christ for Christian living as well as for salvation. Notice the parallel described in Colossians 2:6: "As you have therefore *received* Christ Jesus the Lord, so *walk* in Him." So how did we receive Christ as Lord?—by grace, through faith! And how do we walk in Him (live the Christian life)? Yes, by grace, through faith.

But what does it mean to trust in Christ for soul rest? An illustration comes from the experience of a missionary in Africa, who encountered great difficulty in trying to translate the Gospel of John into the local dialect:

> He faced the problem of finding a word for "believe." He continued to do his best, but always had to leave a blank space when he came to that particular word. Then one day a runner came panting into the camp, having traveled a great distance with a very important message. After blurting out his story, he fell completely exhausted into a nearby hammock. He muttered a brief phrase that seemed to express both his great weariness and his contentment at finding a delightful place of relaxation. The missionary, never having heard these words before, asked a bystander what the runner had said. "Oh, he is saying, 'I'm at the end of myself, therefore I am resting all my weight here!'" The missionary exclaimed, "Praise God! That is the very expression I need for the word 'believe'!" And so he was able to complete his translation.[1]

Even so, we are invited to rest all our weight on Christ as our source of living (Gal. 2:20).

Are we trusting Christ this way? F. B. Meyer identified three conditions for entering "soul rest." *First*, we must take Christ's yoke. First century rabbis referred to their teaching as a yoke that their disciples needed to put on. What was Christ's yoke? He declared "I delight to do your will, O God." (Heb. 10:7; John 8:29). Meyer noted that God's yoke comes to us by His Spirit, by His Word, and by circumstances:

> And I think it is in circumstances that we are most tested. It is just there that we have to meet God, and just as in some electric light the two points have come very close together before the light shines between them, so the point of your will and the point of God's will have to touch, and the light of acquiescence and peace flashes out.[2]

Secondly, Meyer instructs us to trust God fully with the issues of life. The lack of faith in Christ's sufficiency keeps many of us from fully entering into "soul rest." The book of Hebrews uses the example Israel's initial failure to enter Canaan as a type of the disciple who has not come to full dependence upon God for rest:

> There remains therefore a rest for the people of God. For he who has entered His rest has himself also ceased from his works as God did from His. Let us therefore be diligent to enter that rest..." (Heb. 4:9-11).

Although the context serves as a warning for mere professing Christians to ensure that they are true believers, it also points to the principle of resting in the Lord to experience a "milk and honey" quality of life. This is God's intention for us! Christ declared, "I have come that they may have life, and that they may have it more abundantly" (John 10:10).

Meyer describes how whole-hearted trust in God displaces worry:

Do you know what it is when you are worried to kneel down and say to God: "Father, take this" and by one definite act to hand over the worry to God and leave it there? [He then gave this analogy.] Like my dog at home: he used to worry me very much to be fed at dinner, but he never got any food that way. But lately he has adopted something which always conquers me: he sits under the table, and puts one paw on my knee. He never barks, never leaps around, never worries me; I cannot resist the appeal. Although my wife says I must never do it, I keep putting little morsels under the table. Soul, do you know what I am talking about? This is the way to live—with your hand on God's knee. Say, "My God, I am not going to worry; I am not going to fret; but there is my hand, and I wait until the time comes." [3]

Thirdly, Meyer advises us to reckon on God's faithfulness. As Paul wrote to the Corinthians: "God is faithful, by whom you were called into the fellowship of His Son, Jesus Christ our Lord" (1 Cor. 1:9). And the Thessalonians were admonished to trust God for the process of growth in holiness:

Now may the God of peace Himself sanctify you completely; and may your whole spirit, soul, and body be preserved blameless at the coming of our Lord Jesus Christ. He who calls you is faithful, who also will do it" (1 Thess. 5:23,24).

Likewise, Jeremiah found consolation in God's character:

Through the LORD'S mercies we are not consumed,
Because His compassions fail not.
They are new every morning;
great is Your faithfulness.

'The LORD is my portion,' says my soul,
'Therefore I hope in Him!" (Lam. 3:22-24).

God's faithful character verifies His promises.

The discovery of soul rest is illustrated by the testimony of Jack Taylor who came to the end of his strength after striving to be the successful pastor of a large church. He came to appropriate the truth of "Christ in you, the hope of glory" (Col. 1:27). The Holy Spirit then illumined him to appreciate the quality of rest that Jesus promised His weary disciples. Taylor confessed,

> It took me more than twenty years to see the "twofold-edness" of the beautiful passage in Matthew 11:28-30. "Come to Me, all you who labor and are heavy laden, and I will give you rest." There is immediate rest [for salvation] to that one who responds to the Savior's invitation. What a sweet rest it is!...That is the rest of forgiveness...But there is more. "Take My yoke upon you and learn from Me, for I am gentle and lowly in heart, and you will find rest for your souls" (Matt. 11:29). The old time preachers were accustomed to speaking of soul rest. The world is tired and seeking rest today. The rest of forgiveness and the rest of the soul are different qualities. The one depends on coming to Jesus...the other depends on taking the yoke of Jesus...The yoke is a symbol of submission. Some who know Jesus as Savior are not living lives of submission to Him and thus do not have soul rest... Submission is the secret to learning and rest.[4]

As he yielded to God's will and fully depended on Christ as his life, Taylor found refreshing rest for his soul that, in turn, has become an inspiration to many.

Fellow believer, are you weary from trying to fulfill all the "do's" you see as piling higher and higher? Then learn to focus on the one thing needful: Find soul rest.

Full surrender and total confidence in Christ allow that rest to support you. As Paul testified, "I can do all things through Christ who strengthens me" (Phil. 4:13). You are invited to climb into the *hammock* of God's sustaining grace and find rest for your soul!

[1] Our Daily Bread, April 8, 2000. http://www.rbc. org.

[2] F. B. Meyer, *The Christ-Life for the Self-Life*, (Chicago: Moody Press, nd.), 122.

[3] Meyer, 125.

[4] Jack Taylor, *The Key to Triumphant Living*, (Nashville: Broadman Press, 1971), 68, 69.

Blessed Reassurance

Chapter 4
Mixed Emotions

One common cause of spiritual insecurity is an excessive reliance on feelings, particularly when they are negative feelings. A young boy once wrote this note to a psychotherapist:

Dear Dr. Gardener,
What is bothering me is that long ago some big person (it is a boy about 13 years old). He called me *turtle* and I knew he said that because of my plastic surgery. And I think God hates me because of my lip. And when I die He'll probably send me to hell.[1]

This case shows how emotions can drastically affect a person's faith. Let's consider the issue of emotions and their influence in our lives. How should we regard our feelings as we seek to appropriate abundant life in Christ?

First, we *accept the validity* of our emotions. One of the features of being made in God's image is that we have unique personhood which includes emotions (Gen. 1:27). In His perfect humanity, the Lord Jesus experienced and displayed a wide spectrum of feelings. He rejoiced at the salvation of the lost. He wept at the graveside of Lazarus, and He was distraught with the intense pressures of Gethsemane. Jesus expressed indignation at the money changers, frustration with the doubters, compassion for the multitudes, and heart-felt friendship with the apostles. Since Christ, *the Son of Man*, is sinless, we accept His emotions as an appropriate expression of human nature. So we should not consider emotions as insignificant.

Second, we know that emotions can influence us positively or negatively. A *positive* example of emotional influence is recorded in the book of Ezra. After returning from exile in Babylon, the Jewish remnant started to rebuild the temple of the Lord in Jerusalem. (The temple originally constructed by Solomon was destroyed when Jerusalem fell in 587 B.C.) When the people started to rebuild the Temple of the LORD, they displayed a wide spectrum of emotions:

> Then all the people shouted with a great shout, when they praised the LORD, because the foundation of the house of the LORD was laid. But many of the priests and Levities and heads of the fathers' houses, old men who had seen the first temple, wept with a loud voice when the foundation of this temple was laid before their eyes. Yet many shouted aloud for joy, so that the people could not discern the noise of the shout of joy from the noise of the weeping of the people (Ezra 3:11-13).

Their feelings were so varied and intense! Yet, these feelings were influential and expressive in their service to God

The book of Numbers gives a negative example of the influence of emotions. The Israelites wailed in self-pity after hearing the spies' report (telling of the defenses and giants of Canaan:

> So all the congregation lifted up their voices and cried, and the people wept that night. And all the children of Israel complained against Moses and Aaron, and the whole congregation said to them, "If only we had died in the land of Egypt! Or if only we had died in this wilderness! Why has the LORD brought us to

this land to fall by the sword, that our wives and children should become victims? Would it not be better for us to return to Egypt?" (Num. 14:1-3).

In spite of the good reports of Joshua and Caleb, the people's emotional reaction led them to disobey God and refuse to take possession of the Promised Land.

Negative emotions can impact us in assorted ways. High stress situations can trigger irresponsible emotion-based reactions (Judges 11:1-40; 1 Sam 14:24-46). Likewise, the strong feelings of romantic love can draw couples into an intimate relationship before they are prepared to commit to mature, unconditional, marital love. So we acknowledge the real influence of our emotions—for better or for worse.

Third, our emotions should function according to their proper role. This role is similar to the function of nerves in the body. These impulse-carrying fibers carry messages to and from the brain through the spinal cord. Some nerve fibers carry impulses at the rate of 60 to 100 meters per second! Whether these signals are conscious or unconscious, painful or pleasurable, they carry out important functions of communication.[2] Similarly, emotions convey various signals within one's soul.

To use another metaphor, emotions are like the combinations of colors on a palette—whether red, blue, green, yellow or any combination of them. Varying wave lengths of light produce the colors perceived in the eye's retina. Similarly, our emotions express the interplay of our circumstances, our perspective, our values, our choices, our conscience, and our resources—in the soul. They express *how we feel* about things.[3]

There are some "colors" we would prefer to avoid altogether. Physically, for instance, we would probably choose to avoid all the nerve impulses of pain. Yet, Dr. Paul Brand's research has demonstrated how important pain is. He noted that leprosy causes the deadening of the tissue's nerves. This, in turn, removes a vital defense against injuring one's limbs. Before long dreadful physical damage to the body increases because of a lack of pain signals![4]

So what does all this have to do with assurance and abundant living? Frequently, *people experience insecurity because of emotional conflicts.* Perhaps there are troublesome feelings of depression, guilt, fear, anger, or bitterness. Actually these problems shouldn't be blamed on the emotions; usually they're just doing their job! Just as pain sensations tell us to move our hand off a hot stove, these painful emotions sound an internal alarm. The way to resolve these problems is to look to the Lord for His way of resolving these conflicts and frustrations (Matt. 11:28-30).

Finally, what role do your feelings have in a continued life of abiding in Christ? A vital lesson in spiritual growth is to keep emotions *subordinate* to your spirit, your mind, and your will.

The spiritual life is eminently *a life of faith.* This often goes contrary to your emotions which are reacting to a mortal body, a material world, distorted values, and memories. Abraham did not *feel* like offering Isaac on Mt. Moriah, yet he was believing that God would raise his son from the dead if Isaac would be sacrificed (Gen. 22; Heb. 11:17-19). The Lord Jesus didn't *feel* like going to the Cross, but He was obedient to crucifixion and bore all of our sins so we could be redeemed! (Heb. 5:7-9). Likewise, we are summoned to live by faith, not by sight or by feelings (2 Cor. 5:7).

David Tryon wrote of the necessity of living by faith instead of feelings:

> This life which you have entered is all the way along a life of faith. Feelings there will be at times, feelings of joy unutterable and full of glory—but not always. When the feelings come, they will be as the result of

faith, but they are not a necessary part of faith and the lack of them is by no means a proof that faith is in vain. Faith rests, without emotion, on immovable facts, not on feelings which are ever changing. And so for the maintenance of this life, as for its start, for the continual "being filled" with the Spirit as with the first "filling," everything depends on your faith... When circumstances seem impossible, when all signs of grace in you seem at their lowest ebb, when temptation is fiercest, when love and joy and hope seem nearly extinguished in your heart, then cling, without feeling and without emotion, to God's faithfulness; hold on to the fact that He loves you infinitely, and even now is working in you mightily...[5]

Spiritual victory depends on living by faith instead of feelings.

Your emotions must also be subordinate to your mind. Western culture seems to think more through feelings than through logic. This twists one's moral convictions as well. A popular song titled *You Light up My Life* contains the lines, "It can't be wrong, when it feels so right..."

Instead, we are to cast down arguments and every high thing that exalts itself against the knowledge of God, and bring every thought into captivity to the obedience of Christ (2 Cor. 10:5). Like a pilot experiencing vertigo, we need to fly by the "instruments" of God's dependable Word.

To maintain a Christ-centered focus, feelings must be subordinate to your will. You need to choose God's will which is "good, acceptable, and perfect" even when feelings disagree. Hannah W. Smith underlined the importance of keeping the will surrendered to God:

The common thought is, that this life hid with Christ in God is to be lived in the emotions, and consequently all the attention of the soul is directed towards them, and as they are satisfactory or otherwise, the soul rests or is troubled. Now the truth is that this life is not to be lived in the emotions at all, but in the will, and therefore the varying states of emotion do not in the least disturb or affect the reality of the life, if only the will is kept steadfastly abiding in its center, God's will.[6]

God's Word is like the engine of a locomotive, leading the way with faith coming next. Feelings come last, like a caboose on a train.

Remember, God made us with emotions. They are very influential, yet must be under the sway of your renewed conscience, your surrendered will, and your believing mind. The prophet counseled God's people to walk by faith, even when trials come: "Who among you fears the LORD? Who obeys the voice of His Servant? Who walks in darkness And has no light? Let him trust in the name of the LORD And rely upon his God" (Isa. 50:10). Whether you feel like it or not, God loves you, so keep walking by faith.

[1] James Dobson, *Emotions: Can You Trust Them?* (Regal Books, 1980), p. 12 [I corrected the letter's spelling, but not its grammar.]

[2] "Nerve Fiber" in *Mosby's Medical, Nursing, and Allied Health Dictionary.*

[3] These concepts are based upon observations from my counseling experience.

[4] Philip Yancey, *Where is God When it Hurts?*

[5] David Tryon, *But How?* (Moody Press booklet) p. 27,29. Available online at http://www.GraceNotebook under "classics"

[6] Hannah Whitall Smith, *The Christian's Secret of a Happy Life,* (Ages Digital Biblical Library edition-by Rhinosoft Interactive) 46. (Being "happy" is often the byproduct of walking in surrender and trust.)

Blessed Reassurance

Chapter 5
The Good Lawyer

When a man I had begun to counsel was accused of a crime, he turned himself in to the local police station. Bill anticipated signing a document and being released, but instead was arrested and held in the Detention Center. Having no surety for bail, he remained in custody for two months until his trial. One reason for his time behind bars was that he was initially represented by the "duty counsel"—a court appointed lawyer for those who cannot afford one of their own. The duty counsel has earned the reputation of giving somewhat of a lackluster performance, perhaps because of the volume of cases. Visiting Bill at the Detention Center, I heard his frustration at not getting adequate legal help; a lawyer he hired would not have much time for Bill's case because of delays in paper work. Following the trial he was released, quite relieved to be free again.[1]

Although you may not identify with the need for legal defense with a human court, what about God's court? The writer of Hebrews boldly warns of The Lord's sovereign justice:

> For we know Him who said, "Vengeance is Mine, I will repay," says the Lord. And again, "The LORD will judge His people." It is a fearful thing to fall into the hands of the living God (Heb. 10:30,31).

Do you know a good lawyer? Yes, if Jesus is your Savior! He is your defense counsel. "There is therefore now no condemnation to those who are in Christ Jesus" (Rom. 8:1). This is a wonderful consolation! What qualifies the Lord Jesus to represent us as a faithful advocate?

1. Christ's *sinless life* qualifies Him as our advocate.

   "For we do not have a High Priest who cannot sympathize with our weaknesses, but was in all points tempted as we are, yet without sin" (Heb. 4:15).

2. Christ's *death* qualifies Him as our advocate.

   "If anyone sins, we have an Advocate with the Father, Jesus Christ the righteous. And He Himself is the propitiation [substitutionary sacrifice] for our sins, and not for ours only but also for the whole world" (1 John 2:1,2).

3. Christ's *resurrection* qualifies Him as our advocate.

   "Therefore He is also able to save to the uttermost those who come to God through Him, since He always lives to make intercession for them" (Heb. 7:25).

4. Christ's *ascension* qualifies Him as our advocate.

   Romans 8:34 assures us, "Who is he who condemns? It is Christ who died, and furthermore is also risen, who is even at the right hand of God, who also makes intercession for us." Because our Savior has satisfied divine justice by dying in our place, we have a gracious pardon! (Rom. 3:23-26).

   Former president of the Moody Bible Institute, William Culbertson, wrote of the benefits of Christ's ministry in heaven on our behalf:

It is well to remind ourselves that our blessed Saviour is faithful to us in the hour of our great need. Let us not add to Scripture, but let us believe exactly what it says; namely, that "if any man sins, we have an advocate with the Father, Jesus Christ the righteous." Therefore as soon as a child of God has failed, the Lord Jesus is ministering as his Advocate. Such loving ministry should melt our hardened hearts and cause us to live for Him completely. He is our Representative. He is the answer to all the accusations of the devil. The pleading of His blood is the full and final answer to any question concerning the standing of the child of God.[2]

I once was speaking with a brother in Christ who was discovering the Lord Jesus as his Advocate. Although aware that the Enemy is "the accuser of the brethren" (Rev. 12:10), this believer joyfully exclaimed "Christ never loses a case against Satan's accusations!" Amen! We don't just have a "duty counsel"; we have an unfailing Advocate.We also have an intercessor in our hearts. The Holy Spirit indwells every true believer (Eph. 1:13). Find comfort from His spiritual ministry in your life. The Scripture gives this consolation:

Likewise the Spirit also helps in our weaknesses. For we do not know what we should pray for as we ought, but the Spirit Himself makes intercession for us with groanings which cannot be uttered. Now He who searches the hearts knows what the mind of the Spirit is, because He makes intercession for the saints according to the will of God (Rom. 8:26,27).

This hymn of Charles Wesley links the believer's security in Christ to His advocacy for us:

Arise, my soul, arise!
Shake off thy guilty fears;
The bleeding sacrifice,
In my behalf appears.
Before the Throne my Surety stands;
My name is written on His hands.

He ever lives above,
For me to intercede;
His all-redeeming love,
His precious blood to plead.
His blood atoned for all our race,
And sprinkles now the Throne of grace.

My God is reconciled,
His pardoning voice I hear;
He owns me for His child,
I can no longer fear.
With confidence I now draw nigh,
And 'Father, Abba Father' cry.

Give thanks to God that you need not fear the bar of His justice if Christ is your savior and advocate. Rejoice in the blessing of divine intercession on your behalf, and live confidently with this blessed assurance.

[1] This incident took place in Ontario, Canada. The person's name was changed for the sake of anonymity.

[2] William Culbertson, *God's Provision for Holy Living*, 75,76.

Blessed Reassurance

Chapter 6
Your Perception of God

Laura Raney tells the story of a couple of mischievous boys who had a misunderstanding about God:

Two young boys were forever getting into trouble...disrupting classes in school, teasing neighborhood children, taking what didn't belong to them. One day their mother asked the pastor over to see if he could talk some sense into them. Rather than threaten or reprimand them, the pastor decided on a more subtle approach. He would try to help the boys see that God is everywhere, that He is aware of everything and is displeased when they acted wrongly. But the pastor wanted the boys to come to this conclusion on their own, so he began by asking them some questions.

"Young men," he intoned after having the boys sit down, "I have a question for you. Where is God?"

The two boys just sat there, unsure how to answer.

"Where is God?" the preacher repeated, a bit more firmly. "Surely you know that!" The boys remained silent, too frightened to speak.

"I'll ask you one more time," the pastor said, this time even more firmly, "Where is God?"

At that the older boy jumped up and grabbed his brother. "C'mon, let's get out of here!" he whispered. "God's missin' and they think we did it!"[1]

Yes, it's easy to jump to some wrong conclusions about God. The Biblical homework manual of the Minirth-Meyer Clinic notes,

> It seems obvious that there is a connection between our automatic concept of God and the perceptions we have of our natural father or whoever else was a father figure to us in our formative years...The word "father" identifies early in life with what we feel and believe about our earthly father. This perception of God continues, even into adulthood, unless we really dig into God's Word and get to know God intimately.[2]

This observation is substantiated in personal experience and psychological research.

Like the beveled mirrors at an amusement park that make you look 12 feet tall, 3 inches wide, or 3 feet tall, 6 feet wide, our perceptions of God can be severely distorted. To some He is a harsh, austere God who is eager to punish every sin; to others He is like a Santa Clause who knows if you've been bad or good but just sends blessings.

Conference speaker, Mike Wells, once asked those attending the meeting, if it were possible, would they like a personal audience with God in the next room? Many would *not* jump at the chance. Why not? Because—if they stop and consider it—they perceive the Lord to be less than the loving, faithful Father that He really is. This distorted view of God's character throws a wet blanket on the heart's desire to trust and worship Him fully.[3]

Although suffering of human life in a sin-cursed world will seem inconsistent with God's goodness, we must see it in the context of Adam's rebellion and the Fall (Gen. 3). God originally created everything "very good" (Gen. 1:31). Even our Lord Jesus was despised and rejected by the free choices of sinners, yet His tearful prayers in

Gethsemane were answered through the Cross, His bodily resurrection, and ascension (Heb 5:7-9; Matt 26:39; Phil 2:6-11). By His sacrifice, all true believers will experience God's eternal goodness! (1 Pet. 1:3-5). The author of *The Christian's Secret of a Happy Life* observed the need to honestly evaluate our concept of God.

It is of vital importance now and then to drag out our secret thoughts and feelings about the Lord into the full light of the Holy Spirit, that we may see what our attitude about Him really is. It is fatally easy to get into the habit of wrong thoughts about God, thoughts which will insensibly separate us from Him by a wide gulf of doubt and unbelief. More than anything else, more than sin, wrong thoughts about God sap the foundations of our spiritual life, and grieve His heart of love. We can understand this from ourselves. Nothing grieves us so much as to have our friends misjudge and misunderstand us, and attribute to us motives we scorn. And nothing, I believe, so grieves the Lord.[4]

Consider the primary roles of your earthly father to protect and provide for you. If he did not fulfill these responsibilities, whether intentionally or unintentionally, there would likely be a natural tendency to doubt the heavenly Father's nature as protector and provider.

Perhaps this extends to the mother's role also. Since a child looks to its mom for love and nurture, if these qualities were noticeably missing, could there be a reluctance to trust God's love and support?

How can we correct our view of God? This primarily involves renewing our mind through the Scriptures. As Paul exhorted the Romans, "And do not be conformed to this world, but be transformed by the renewing of your mind, that you may prove what is that good and acceptable and perfect will of God" (Rom. 12:2).

For example, one of the qualities that is most reassuring to us is God's *goodness.* Consider these verses from Psalms:

Good and upright is the LORD;
Therefore He teaches sinners in the way...
[God] loves righteousness and justice;
The earth is full of the goodness of the LORD...
Oh, taste and see that the LORD is good;
Blessed is the man who trusts in Him!
You are good, and do good;
Teach me Your statutes"
    (Psalm 25:8 33:5; 34:8; 119:68).

And the prophets declared,

I will mention the lovingkindnesses of the LORD
And the praises of the LORD,
According to all that the LORD has bestowed on us,
And the great goodness toward the house of Israel,
Which He has bestowed on them according to His mercies,
According to the multitude of His lovingkindnesses...
The LORD is good, A stronghold in the day of trouble;
And He knows those who trust in Him"
    (Isaiah 63:7; Nahum 1:7).

To deny God's goodness is the essence of unbelief, since Paul warns, "do you despise the riches of His goodness, forbearance, and longsuffering, not knowing that the goodness of God leads you to repentance?" (Rom. 2:4).

Hannah W. Smith recalled the difference such biblical renewal made in her fellowship with God:

I shall never forget the hour when I first discovered that God was really good. I had, of course, always known that the Bible said He was good, but I had thought that He was religiously good; it had never dawned on me that it meant that He was actually and practically good, with the same kind of goodness He has commanded us to have...And then one day I came in my reading of the Bible across the words, "O taste and see that the Lord is good," and suddenly they meant something...And I saw that, since God is omniscient, He must know what is the best and highest good of all, and that therefore His goodness must necessarily be beyond question.[5]

Perhaps you have been taught correct doctrine about God's attributes, but this hasn't sunk down into your heart. A helpful strategy to restore an appreciation of God's goodness is to read the Gospels with special attention to the qualities of the Lord Jesus. The New Testament draws attention to Christ's unique role in revealing our Creator:

God...has in these last days spoken to us by His Son, whom He has appointed heir of all things, through whom also He made the worlds; who [is] the brightness of His glory and the express image of His person, and upholding all things by the word of His power..." (Heb. 1:2-4).

J. B. Phillips confirmed how Christ's manifestation of God's character enlarges our perception of who God really is:

We can never have too big a concept of God, and the more scientific knowledge (in whatever field) advances, the greater becomes our idea of His vast and complicated wisdom. Yet, unless we are to remain befogged and bewildered, and give up all hope of ever knowing God as a Person, we have to accept His own planned focusing of Himself in a human being, Jesus Christ.[6]

Think of the One who opened the eyes of the blind, gave the leper that healing touch, fed the 5,000, rebuked the false teachers, cleansed the Temple, invited the little children to come to Him, calmed stormy seas and frightened hearts, wept at the grave side of His friend Lazarus and raised him from the dead, who laid down His life for us. These reveal wonderful qualities of God's character!

As we renounce false ideas about God and affirm true characteristics of Him, we find truth that sets us free! (John 8:32). We then increasingly love Him, because He first loved us (1 John 4:19). Insecurity based on a harsh view of God gives way to peaceful confidence in His virtue. So, cultivate a heart for God. Regain an accurate perception of His attributes and echo the faith of Jeremiah:

Through the LORD'S mercies we are not consumed,
Because His compassions fail not.
They are new every morning;
Great is Your faithfulness.
"The LORD is my portion," says my soul,
"Therefore I hope in Him!" (Lam. 3:22-24).

[1] Rusty Wright and Linda Raney Wright, *500 Clean Jokes and Humorous Stories* (Urichsville, OH: Barbour, 1985), 205,06.

[2] Frank Minirth, Paul Meier, Richard Meier, and Don Hawkins, *The Healthy Christian Life*, (Grand Rapids: Baker, 1988), p 77. Like other sciences, psychology—when correctly interpreted—can be of value in gaining information (general revelation) for diagnostic use, however, God's Word alone has the answer for man's ultimate problems (2 Tim 3:16,17).

[3] Michael Wells' ministry is located online at www. abidinglife.org.

[4] Hannah Whitall Smith, *The God Who is Enough*, (Chicago: Moody Press), 97,98. Emphasis added.

[5] Smith, 94-95.

[6] J.B. Phillips, *Your God is Too Small*, (Wyvern), 124.

Blessed Reassurance

Chapter 7
Freedom from Guilt

A guilty conscience is one of the *weights* that the runner must *lay aside* in the Christian race (Heb. 12:1). The shadow of guilt is another reason why believers need reassurance concerning their salvation. The apostle Paul wrote to his son in the faith, "Now the purpose of the commandment is love from a pure heart, from a *good conscience*, and from sincere faith" (1 Tim. 1:5).

The following questions and biblical quotations summarize the reality of total forgiveness for the child of God. For further benefit, pray over these passages and journal your observations and insights.

1. How do you gain God's righteousness?

   "Therefore, having been justified [declared righteous] by faith, we have peace with God through our Lord Jesus Christ" (Rom. 5:1).

   "There is therefore now no condemnation to those who are in Christ Jesus" (Rom. 8:1).

2. Who purchased your righteousness?

   "For He [God the Father] made Him [the Son] who knew no sin to be sin for us, that we might become the righteousness of God in Him" (2 Cor. 5:21).

3. How many of our sins were judicially pardoned through your salvation?

"And you, being dead in your trespasses and the uncircumcision of your flesh, He has made alive together with Him, *having forgiven you all trespasses*, having wiped out the handwriting of requirements that was against us, which was contrary to us. And He has taken it out of the way, having nailed it to the cross (Col. 2:13,14).

4. Does God want to cleanse His children of their failures?

"Come now, and let us reason together," Says the LORD, "Though your sins are like scarlet, They shall be as *white* as snow; Though they are red like crimson, They shall be as *wool*" (Isaiah 1:18).

"But if we walk in the light as He is in the light, we have fellowship with one another, and the blood of Jesus Christ His Son cleanses us from all sin" (1 John 1:7).

5. What blessings do you have in Christ?

"But of Him you are in Christ Jesus, who became for us wisdom from God—and righteousness and sanctification and redemption—that, as it is written, "He who glories, let him glory in the LORD" (1 Cor. 1:30,31).

6. What is your new spiritual identity?

"But you are a chosen generation, a royal priesthood, a holy nation, His own special people, that you may proclaim the praises of Him who called you out of darkness into His marvelous light; who once were not a people but are now the people of God, who had not obtained mercy but now have obtained mercy" (1 Pet. 2:9,10).

7. What should be your attitude toward the past?

"Not that I have already attained, or am already perfected; but I press on, that I may lay hold of that for which Christ Jesus has also laid hold of me. Brethren, I do not count myself to have apprehended; but one thing I do, *forgetting those things which are behind* and reaching forward to those things which are ahead, I press toward the goal for the prize of the upward call of God in Christ Jesus" (Phil. 3:11-14).

Divine favor is not a license for intentional wrongdoing; grace draws us into God's love and motivates cooperative obedience. Christ declared, "He who has My commandments and keeps them, it is he who loves Me. And he who loves Me will be loved by My Father, and I will love him and manifest Myself to him" (John 14:21).

With a clear conscience your sense of assurance is fortified. Sometimes, however, emotion-based guilt may linger. Then, faith must grasp the sufficiency of Christ's finished work. Love will be expressed by such faith. The apostle John counseled, "By this we shall know we are of the truth and shall assure our hearts before Him. For if our heart condemns us, God is greater than our heart, and knows all things" (1 John 3:19,20).

To maintain a clear conscience, stay focused on your union with Christ (John 15:1-8). Embrace the Cross and confess known sins (Luke 9:23; 1 John 1:9). Accept God's cleansing by faith, and forgive yourself! The light of God's grace will displace the shadows of guilt.

Blessed Reassurance

Chapter 8
Choosing God's Best

When our twin sons were nine years old, they were on the same soccer team. In that junior soccer league, they learned about the sport and got a good work out. A first place finish for their team capped an exciting play off. I appreciated how their two coaches accepted the players at their level of ability, yet motivated them to do their best.

As children of God—on His "team"—what motivates us to be our best for God here and now? If our salvation is secure, how are we still accountable? Considering the amazing grace of God that saves and keeps us, "Shall we continue in sin that grace may abound?" (Rom 6:1). The immediate and emphatic answer is *absolutely not*! Let's consider three basic motivations that inspire us to say "no" to sin patterns and "yes" to God's good will.

First, we are motivated to live for God because *we are under His providential training*. In other words, if the believer stubbornly disobeys, God will bring discipline into his/her life. The writer of Hebrews, quoting Proverbs, reminds us:

> "For whom the LORD loves He chastens, And scourges every son whom He receives." If you endure chastening, God deals with you as with sons; for what son is there whom a father does not chasten? Furthermore, we have had human fathers who corrected us, and we paid them respect. Shall we not much more readily be in subjection to the Father of spirits and live? (Heb. 12:6,7,9; 1 Cor. 11:29-32).

We need a clear understanding of God's discipline. Not all trials are sent to correct disobedience. Remember Job. When chastening comes, it should be perceived as corrective, not punitive. Consider the importance of this distinction:

> The sharp difference [between punishment and discipline] can be seen in both the attitude and the goal of the one doing it. The attitude behind punishment is anger and indignation, and its goal is justice; the attitude behind discipline is love, and its goal is the benefit and development of the person. A total contrast! And the crucial application to us is knowing that GOD, under the new covenant, never deals with his children on the basis of punishment. All of the punishment of God for our sins was fully received by Christ on the cross.[1]

A joyful fellow believer once said to me, "When I was a boy, I was given an ice cream cone when I pleased my parents. I now love to please my Heavenly Father, because I like getting His ice cream cones [blessings]." Although new covenant believers have already been given "every spiritual blessing," we intuitively desire to please the Father (Eph. 1:3).

Another aspect of God's providential training is the sowing and reaping principle. Galatians 6:7 warns:

> Do not be decived, God is not mocked; for whatever a man sows, that he will aslo reap.

Although God totally pardons His redeemed ones, the alcoholic is not exempted from liver damage, nor is the compulsive spender protected from financial problems. The sexually immoral is not protected from STDs, nor is the "saved" criminal excused from the court's verdict.

The one who ignores God's moral absolutes does not just break the law, he breaks *himself* on the law.

The second motivator for living for God as a believer is the *Judgment Seat of Christ.* The apostle Paul referred to this event in 2 Corinthians 5:9,10:

> Therefore we make it our aim, whether present or absent, to be well pleasing to Him. For we must all appear before the judgment seat of Christ, that each one may receive the things done in the body, according to what he has done, whether good [rewardable] or bad [useless].

This evaluation will occur when Christ comes for His own. In heaven, believers will stand at the Judgment Seat of Christ and receive rewards (for righteous and loving works) or loss of reward (for unrighteous and vain works (1 Cor. 3:10-15). This judgment does not determine your destiny. Your destiny is determined by having salvation—having your name in the *Lamb's book of life* (Phil. 4:3; Rev. 21:27).

Does it appear to be selfish to live a good life in order to be rewarded by God? Although obedience has intrinsic rewards in this life (Rom. 12:2), future rewards are valued in the teaching of the Lord Jesus:

> But you, when you pray, go into your room, and when you have shut your door, pray to your Father who is in the secret place; and your Father who sees in secret will reward you openly" (Matt. 6:6).

Self concern is not necessarily wrong; we naturally care about our own welfare (Eph. 5:29).

Our perspective about the motivational value of future rewards should correspond to the action of the twenty four elders in the book of Revelation: "[They] fall down before Him who sits on the throne and worship Him who lives forever and ever, and cast their crowns before the throne..." (Rev. 4:10). Our ultimate goal is to glorify God, from whom all blessings flow!

Thirdly, Christ's disciples want to be used of God for noble purposes in this life. We recognize the value of God's Kingdom (Col. 1:14). Although much of daily life may seem mundane and meaningless, serving as an ambassador of Christ is eternally significant (2 Cor. 5:20). To be effectively used of God, we need to be walking in harmony with God, sensitive to His will. Paul exhorted Timothy to live with a clean conscience so as to be available for God's holy ministry:

> But in a great house there are not only vessels of gold and silver, but also of wood and clay, some for honor and some for dishonor. Therefore if anyone *cleanses himself* from the latter, he will be a vessel for honor, sanctified and useful for the Master, *prepared for every good work.* Flee also youthful lusts; but pursue righteousness, faith, love, peace with those who call on the Lord out of a pure heart (2 Tim. 2:20-22).

Like Timothy, the one saved by grace is motivated by the desire to be fruitful. However, a disobedient believer, grieving and quenching God's Spirit, will likely forfeit opportunities of being used by God to make a difference in the lives of others.[2]

Finally, the ultimate motivator for us as believers is *loving gratitude* to our gracious God. The apostle Paul testified:

> For the love of Christ compels us, because we judge thus: that if One died for all, then all died; and He died for all, that those who live should live no longer for themselves, but for Him who died for them and rose again (2 Cor. 5:14,15).

If we love Christ, we will obey Him for God's glory and our good (John 14:15).

You can add to this list when you consider the wisdom and benefits of choosing God's best for your life day by day. These motivations must have captured the heart of Joachim Neander who wrote, *Praise to the Lord, the Almighty.* Stanza two declares:

> Praise to the Lord,
> Who o'er all things so wondrously reigneth,
> Shelters thee under His wings,
> Yea, so gently sustaineth!
> Hast thou not seen
> How thy desires all have been
> Granted in what He ordaineth?

Instead of fostering a carnal lifestyle, these biblical motivations demonstrate how believers are still accountable to their Heavenly Father. Assurance and security do not minimize your incentives for pleasing God here and now. A lifestyle of seeking to please our Redeemer confirms the genuineness of your faith and calls you to invest your time for eternal values.

[1] Bob George, *Classic Christianity*, (Eugene, OR: Harvest House, 1989) 194 (original emphasis).

[2] These biblical allusions indicate that, although Christians can never lose their relationship with God (Rom. 5:1), they may hinder their fellowship with Him (Eph. 4:30; 1 Thess. 5:19; 1 Pet. 3:7b). Some are now using these terms interchangeably, since there is an overlap in meaning—the believer can never hinder fellowship to the extent of nullifying the relationship (1 Cor. 1:9). Yet the risen Christ's rebukes to the churches in Asia Minor in Revelation 2:1-3:22 indicate that fellowship, intimacy, and usefulness can be hindered by the willful sins and unfaithfulness of the churches. See chapter 16.

PART 2

Studies on *Reassurance*

Blessed Reassurance

Chapter 9
The Roots of Insecurity

One of the important foundations for a healthy, vital Christian life is the assurance of your salvation. It is nearly impossible to have Christ as the center of your life if you're not sure He is *in* your life as personal Savior (John 1:12).

Many believers who struggle with uncertainty regarding their standing with God could progress to assurance if they could discern the causes of their *insecurity*. Let's consider some common factors that may hinder a true believer's sense of assurance.

1. Insecurity Due to Feeling Unsaved

Sometimes the nature of the believer's insecurity is more of an emotional issue than a doctrinal or spiritual one. In other words, there is a difference between *feeling* unsaved and *doubting* God's promises of redemption.

For example, when a person is raised in an atmosphere of performance-based acceptance or blatant rejection, this causes emotional damage in childhood. Although parental love should be an expression and symbol of the Heavenly Father's love and faithfulness, this family love is often lacking or not expressed meaningfully. Therefore, when the rejected person becomes born again through faith in Christ, he/she may lack the emotional confirmation that he/she is truly accepted by the ultimate Parent—God.

In a counseling session, Dr. Charles Solomon had a veteran missionary come for help because she suffered from a chronic lack of assurance. This sister had a clear Christian testimony, a strong grasp of scriptural promises, had led many to Christ, and appreciated the doctrines of grace. In light of her background and rejection patterns growing up, Dr. Solomon challenged her to consider that she did not doubt her salvation; instead, she *felt* unsaved. When she distinguished the emotional component from her spiritual life, she was enabled to understand and eventually resolve this uncertainty.[1]

The apostle John affirmed, "For if our heart condemns us, God is greater than our heart, and knows all things. Beloved, if our heart does not condemn us, we have confidence toward God" (1 John 3:20,21). Emotional healing comes as we experience divine and human love and acceptance over time. God's assurance to His prophet applies to each one of His children: "The LORD has appeared of old to me, saying: 'Yes, I have loved you with an everlasting love; Therefore with lovingkindness I have drawn you'" (Jer. 31:3).

Biblical faith is not based on feelings—whether positive or negative—so we should recognize the possibility of emotional resistance to feeling saved. In spite of misleading emotions, the believer can have confidence that salvation in Christ has been received and will be kept by God. Paul's assurance rose above circumstances and distractions:

> For this reason I also suffer these things; nevertheless I am not ashamed, for I know whom I have believed and am persuaded that He is able to keep what I have committed to Him until that Day (2 Tim. 1:12).

2. Insecurity Due to Legalism

Legalism involves legislating ideal behaviors, trying to gain practical righteousness by self-effort, and focusing on externals more than the heart motives. The Galatian church fell into this trap due to false teachers:

> O foolish Galatians! Who has bewitched you that you should not obey the truth, before whose eyes Jesus Christ was clearly portrayed among you as crucified? This only I want to learn from you: Did you receive the Spirit by the works of the law, or by the hearing of faith? Are you so foolish? Having begun in the Spirit, are you now being made perfect by the flesh? (Gal. 3:1-3).

These believers had been saved by grace through faith, but later had been duped into trying to complete their salvation by attempting to keep the law of Moses.

They were also seeking to grow spiritually by trying to keep external standards in their own strength. Their view of Christian living needed a grace awakening. The apostle affirmed,

> For we through the Spirit eagerly wait for the hope of righteousness by faith. For in Christ Jesus neither circumcision nor uncircumcision avails anything, but faith working through love (Gal. 5:5,6).

Whether obvious or subtle, legalism can become a root of insecurity.

To the extent that Christians "keep the rules" they will be tempted to have pride and make comparisons. Or, if they fail to live up to these rules, they will be burdened by guilt and condemnation. This feeling of estrangement from God raises questions as to whether the disciple is really saved after all: "If I were truly saved, wouldn't I be more obedient? More consistent? More victorious?"

The most comprehensive description of the legalist's inner struggle is found in the seventh chapter of Romans. Although a detailed exposition of the chapter cannot be explored here, some essential observations can help to navigate this passage. Remember that Romans chapter five explains the nature of justification by faith and chapter six teaches identification with Christ by faith.[2] However, before a fuller statement of the victory of faith through the Spirit-filled life (chapter 8), Paul is guided to convey the frustration all believers recognize: "For what I am doing, I do not understand. For what I will to do, that I do not practice; but what I hate, that I do" (Rom. 7:15).

Paul speaks of an earlier time in his life as a present conviction.[3] To the extent that a Christian lives according the flesh, he will find himself feeling that "...I am carnal, sold under sin" (Rom. 7:14b). This condition is intensified when a believer tries to live a holy life by means of external standards in his/her own strength. This legalistic paradox drags the frustrated Christian to the point of despair and misery: "O wretched man that I am! Who will deliver me from this body of death?" (Rom. 7:24).

Thankfully, the way of deliverance is explained in the passages surrounding this "page from Paul's journal." Those who are in Christ are totally forgiven and justified! "Therefore, having been justified by faith, we have peace with God through our Lord Jesus Christ...There is therefore now no condemnation to those who are in Christ Jesus..." (Rom. 5:1; 8:1). From this assured standing the disciple is to walk according to the Spirit and live out of his/her union with

Christ by grace through faith! We have been freed from sin's authority through our union with Christ: "For the law of the Spirit of life in Christ Jesus has made me free from the law of sin and death" (Rom. 8:2).

Therefore, if you have been burdened by the weight of legalism, realize that this is no proof that you're unsaved. Rather, the law has magnified the sinful tendencies of your flesh: "For I know that in me (that is, in my flesh) nothing good dwells..." (Rom 7:18a). The flesh, however, is distinct from your new human spirit where you are unified with Christ.[4]

When you are born again, you agree with Paul in your spirit: "For I delight in the law of God according to the inward man" (Rom. 7:22). In the Grace Economy, *assurance is not a license to sin, but an incentive to respond in loving gratitude to God.* Motivated from this secure relationship, "His commandments are not burdensome" (1 John 5:3b). "For sin shall not have dominion over you, for you are not under law but under grace" (Rom. 6:14).

So instead of maintaining a holding pattern of insecurity and doubt due to legalism and guilt, base your assurance on God's promises and move ahead by walking in the Holy Spirit's fellowship and power.

3. Insecurity Due to Carnal Confusion

When born again believers walk "according to the flesh," doubts may arise in their mind as to whether or not they have lost their salvation or if they are truly regenerate.[5]

One reason for this is that the Holy Spirit is grieved and quenched by intentional sin in a believer's life. The whisper of His inner witness is muffled by the interference of the world, guilt, and the devil. Since God's Spirit seeks to witness with our spirit

65

that we are "sons of God," lack of fellowship with Him may hinder the disciple's perception of this inner witness (Rom. 8:16; Eph. 4:30; 1 Thess. 5:19).

Fear concerning Biblical warnings can also be a source of confusion. 1 Corinthians 6:9,10 cautions,

> Do you not know that the unrighteous will not inherit the kingdom of God? Do not be deceived. Neither fornicators, nor idolaters, nor adulterers, nor homosexuals, nor sodomites, nor thieves, nor covetous, nor drunkards, nor revilers, nor extortioners will inherit the kingdom of God.

This warning is a valid motivation for the backslider to verify if he/she truly has truly been redeemed: "Examine yourselves as to whether you are in the faith. Test yourselves. Do you not know yourselves, that Jesus Christ is in you?—unless indeed you are disqualified" (2 Cor. 13:5).

When people receive Christ as Lord and Savior by grace through faith, their spirit becomes alive toward God; their essential nature expresses God's indwelling life (2 Pet. 1:4; 2 Cor. 5:17). Paul continued,

> And such [characterized by sin] were some of you. But you were washed, but you were sanctified, but you were justified in the name of the Lord Jesus and by the Spirit of our God (1 Cor. 6:11).

Yet, some have concluded that any incident or temporary pattern of former fleshly sins prove that the person is unsaved. The defeated person becomes confused: "Am I born again and backslidden, or unsaved?"

Is it possible for a regenerate child of God to walk according to the flesh? Scripture and experience indicate that a carnal condition (in the soul/

actions) is, sadly, a common problem. Yet, neither is carnality "normal" for saints! In the letter to the church at Corinth, the apostle rebukes the believers for fleshly behavior such as divisions, sexual immorality, lawsuits against fellow Christians, insensitivity to the scruples of others, and disrespect for the Communion service (1 Cor. 1:10-17; 5:1-13; 6:1-11; 8:1-13; 11:17-32). This, however, was not an indication that the church was mostly unregenerate; rather, that they had been influenced by their corrupt culture to walk after the flesh instead of according to their new nature (1 Cor. 1:2).

Notice how Paul rebuked the carnality of the congregation:

> And I, brethren, could not speak to you as to spiritual people but as to *carnal*, as to babes in Christ. I fed you with milk and not with solid food; for until now you were not able to receive it, and even now you are still not able; for *you are still carnal*. For where there are envy, strife, and divisions among you, are you not *carnal* and behaving like mere men? (1 Cor. 3:1-3).

Their temporary carnality did not indicate that they were unsaved (as the "natural man" in 2:14); it demonstrated that they had not grown spiritually and were not filled with the Holy Spirit.[6]

The true believer is not in the flesh positionally, but has the capacity to walk according to the flesh. This disobedience would lead to God's corrective discipline (Heb. 12:6-9; Rom. 8:9; 1 Pet. 2:11).[7]

In summary, carnal confusion arises when the believer walks intentionally or passively *according to the flesh*. This, however, does not prove that the carnal Christian is unsaved. For these Corinthians, the remedy was not re-conversion, but growth and sanctification (Rom. 6:1-23).

Don't let carnality ensnare you! If it does, repent and claim the power of the cross of Christ (Gal. 5:24). Rather than losing your assurance, reaffirm your faith and allow your security in Christ to motivate you to *walk according to the Spirit.*

[1] For further information on the effects of a lack of meaningful love, see Charles Solomon, *The Ins and Out of Rejection* (Sevierville, TN: Solomon Publications).

[2] For an exposition of these chapters of Romans see Robert Jones, *The Gospel for the Believer* at www.gracenotebook.com.

[3] This struggle was probably part of Paul's three year sabbatical in Arabia after his conversion (Gal. 1:17). Paul's testimony as a Spirit-filled apostle is that he lived an exemplary life with a clear conscience (1 Cor. 4:16; 11:1; Acts 23:1; 2 Tim. 1:3). Others (such as Frank Humphrey) interpret this chapter as referring to Paul's pre-conversion experience. Some assert that the struggle pertains to both Christian and non-Christians as they attempt to contend with the flesh, under the law, apart from grace. See W. H. Griffith Thomas, *St. Paul's Epistle to the Romans*, Wm. B. Eerdmans, 1956, 191-94.

[4] Technically, the flesh is not a co-equal nature, but the body and soul's residual patterns and tendencies from the crucified "old man." The flesh is in you, but it's not you. This is not hair splitting, but significant, since Paul went on to declare, "Now if I do what I will not to do, it is no longer I who do it, but sin that dwells in me" (Rom. 7:20). This doesn't excuse the believer from personal responsibility. Rather, this distinction reveals the true source of spiritual opposition—the Sin principle (Rom. 7:17). This principle results from the world/flesh/devil influence that opposes the Holy Spirit's ministry in your life. Thankfully, in Christ believers have been set free from the law of sin and death through the resources of the abundant life—Christ in you, the hope of glory (Rom. 8:2; Col. 1:27). The "old man" was co-crucified with Christ (Rom. 6:6) and is no longer your nemesis (Col. 3:9).

See GraceNotebook.com "definition of terms" and David Needham's analysis of the differences between the flesh and the old man in *Birthright.*

⁵ "Flesh" in this context is the interface of the mortal body and human soul that consists of the beliefs, values, identity messages, and coping mechanisms acquired through living independently of God. It is sin-stained (by depravity from Adam) and sin-trained (from each person's life experiences and choices—Rom. 7:18; Gal.5:16-21). "Carnal" (Latin root) is another word for "fleshly" (Rom. 8:6,7).

⁶ The fullness of the Spirit is God's will for every Christian: "And do not be drunk with wine, in which is dissipation; but be filled with the Spirit" (Eph. 5:18). This is a command, which implies that believers may or may not—at a given time—be under the full influence of the indwelling Holy Spirit. We have all of Him, but does He have all of us?

⁷ This treatment of the "carnal Christian" by no means legitimizes sin as an acceptable lifestyle for disciples of Christ. Many professing Christians bear no fruit, live a perpetually carnal lifestyle and seek false refuge under the banner of the "carnal Christian." Such ones are tragically assuming that intellectual assent about Christ guarantees heaven, even if there are no vital signs (contra James 2:14-26, see chapter 11).

However, just as it is wrong to legitimize the "carnal Christian" as an acceptable lifestyle, so it is unbiblical to deny the possibility of a temporary backslidden condition in the regenerate (1 Cor. 3:1-4). Too often, redeemed ones wander in the wilderness of self and sinful habits for years, like the nation of Israel did (Num. 14-36). They have life, but not abundant, victorious life (John 10:10). When full surrender to God is joined by a personal reckoning of one's identification with Christ by faith, Promised Land living can be experienced (Rom. 12:1; Gal. 2:20).

Blessed Reassurance

Chapter 10
The Roots of Insecurity
(Continued)

We have considered some issues that may jeopordize a believer's confidence in his/her salvation. In this chapter we examine three more.

4. Insecurity Due to Faith in Faith

Have you ever doubted your salvation because your conversion experience was less sensational than someone else's? I recall in my teenage years being awed by testimonies of some who had been notorious rascals for decades and then were gloriously saved. Although I rejoice in the way God redeems such lives, I felt inferior. I had received Christ at about seven years of age—too early to get into major trouble. Yet, the Lord delights in the salvation of young people (Matt. 19:13,14). Those who have spent many prodigal years are usually candid about their regrets. If they had come to Christ earlier, many of their scars could have been avoided.

The apostle Paul glorified God in his testimony of salvation:

Although I was formerly a blasphemer, a persecutor, and an insolent man; but I obtained mercy because I did it ignorantly in unbelief. And the grace of our Lord was exceedingly abundant, with faith and love which are in Christ Jesus. This is a faithful saying and worthy of all acceptance, that Christ

Jesus came into the world to save sinners, of whom I am chief. However, for this reason I obtained mercy, that in me first Jesus Christ might show all longsuffering, as a pattern to those who are going to believe on Him for everlasting life. Now to the King eternal, immortal, invisible, to God who alone is wise, be honor and glory forever and ever. Amen (1 Tim. 1:13-17; Acts 9:1-22).

After meeting the risen Christ on the road to Damascus, Saul the persecutor became Paul the apostle.

Timothy's redemption was less sensational. The apostle reminded him,

I call to remembrance the genuine faith that is in you, which dwelt first in your grandmother Lois and your mother Eunice, and I am persuaded is in you also...and that from childhood you have known the Holy Scriptures, which are able to make you wise for salvation through faith which is in Christ Jesus" (2 Tim. 1:5;3:15; Acts 16:1-3).

Paul's conversion experience was much different than that of his young apprentice, yet both were equally genuine. Even so, your testimony doesn't need to mimic someone else's experience in order to be real.

Sometimes insecurity is caused by focusing on one's *faith* rather than on *the Lord Jesus Himself.* Remember, God saves us by grace: "For by grace you have been saved through faith, and that not of yourselves; it is the gift of God, not of works, lest anyone should boast" (Eph. 2:8,9). What's the difference? If you're trusting in the strength of your faith, doubts will shake the security of your relationship with Christ. However, if you are trusting Christ's finished work and relying fully on Him as personal Lord and Savior, your assurance is based on Him!

Don't revel in the strength of your belief, but in the faithfulness of God in Christ: "Therefore He is also able to save to the uttermost those who come to God through Him, since He always lives to make intercession for them" (Heb. 7:25). Thankfully, the Holy Spirit convicts us of our need and enables us to place our faith in Christ (1 Cor. 12:3). Even faith that is as small as a mustard seed lays hold of so great a salvation when it springs from a heart of repentance (Luke 17:6; 2 Tim. 1:12).

Insecurity due to weak faith is not necessarily resolved by rehearsing the plan of salvation. That's why the writer of Hebrews did not repeat the "A B C's" of the gospel to challenge those wavering believers. Instead, the letter advanced to deeper truth that would motivate the Hebrew Christians to take refuge in the Jesus the Messiah, to persevere and grow in their New Covenant faith (Heb. 6:1-9, see chapter 13).

By way of contrast, some evangelists seem intent on stirring up some degree of insecurity in the audience in order to call for an invitation that would "really" save them (no matter how much evidence there has been of their devotion to Christ). Although this may make the evangelist's meeting appear more successful, in reality believers may just be circling back to their initial profession of faith. They try a more sincere conversion prayer instead of appropriating spiritual victory over the self-life (Rom. 6:6-14). This cycle of repeated sinner's prayers reinforces insecurity rather than promoting valid assurance (John 10:27-29).

The value of faith depends on the *object* of faith. Instead of faith in faith, we need to trust the faithfulness of God in Christ!

Imagine people doubting that they are alive because they had misplaced their birth certificate. That would be paranoia, right? The best evidence of new life is *growth*: "But grow in the grace and knowledge of our Lord and Savior Jesus Christ. To Him be the glory both now and forever. Amen" (2 Pet. 3:18).

5. Insecurity Due to Uncertainty about Election

One of the most incomprehensible aspects of redemption is the antinomy of the sovereignty of God and the responsibility of man. Although space does not allow us to delve into the arguments for/against Calvinism or Arminianism, the confusion about election and predestination has caused many to be uncertain about their salvation.

The Calvinist theologian probably assumes that his doctrine encourages personal assurance. For example, L. Boettner wrote this about the implications of election:

All true Christians may and should know that they are among those who have been predestinated unto eternal life. Since faith in Christ, which is a gift from God, is the means of salvation, and since this is not given to any but the elect only, the person who knows that he has this faith can be assured that he is among the elect.[8]

The five point Calvinist reasons that since regeneration precedes salvation, and faith is only granted to those chosen and called according to God's decree, so believers should take their faith as an assurance of salvation.[9] However, Reformed theologians point to another crucial aspect of evidence—good works (holiness). 2 Peter 1:10 draws this kind of conclusion: "Therefore, brethren, be even more diligent to make your call and election sure, for if you do these things you will never stumble." The preceding context points to the need for virtue, knowledge, self-control, perseverance, godliness, brotherly kindness, and love. Boettner quoted Mozley as stating,

> Good works become the mark and test of election, and when taken in the comprehensive sense in which Peter is here thinking of them, they are the only marks and tests of election.[10]

I grant that there is a consistency of logic in this model, however, not a few believers from this doctrinal heritage are troubled with insecurity regarding their salvation. They may wonder, "What if my good works don't adequately confirm that I am chosen? If my election does not involve my responsibility, what if I haven't been included? Do my moral/spiritual failures indicate that I am merely religious and, instead, predestined to hell?"

Although sincere, godly scholars have debated these issues for centuries, the following clarifications safeguard the New Testament perspective on assurance and security.

An Open Invitation

The anxious believer needs to focus on the wonderful invitations of Scripture that are as genuine as they sound. Christ proclaims,

> *Come to Me*, all you who labor and are heavy laden, and I will give you rest. Take My yoke upon you and learn from Me, for I am gentle and lowly in heart, and you will find rest for your souls. For My yoke is easy and My burden is light (Matt. 11:28-30). And the Spirit and the bride say, "Come!" And let him who hears say, "Come!" And let him who thirsts come.

Whoever desires, let him take the water of life freely (Rev. 22:17).[11]

The validity of this gracious invitation is supported by the declared desire of God, "who desires all men to be saved and to come to the knowledge of the truth" (1 Tim. 2:4; 2 Pet. 3:9).

A Sufficient Atonement

A Calvinist professor instructed pastoral counselors to avoid saying to a non-Christian that "Christ died for you," because it cannot be known that the counselee is among the elect (reflecting the belief that Christ died only for the elect).[12] This belief in limited atonement—although logically defended in the Reformed paradigm—has also been interpreted in a way that undermines world missions and raises doubts concerning assurance in the struggling believer.[13] However, the apostle John declared,

My little children, these things I write to you, so that you may not sin. And if anyone sins, we have an Advocate with the Father, Jesus Christ the righteous. And He Himself is the propitiation for our sins, and not for ours only but also *for the whole world* (1 John 2:1,2).

Dear reader, God does love you; and Christ did die on Calvary on your behalf! Therefore, take refuge in Him.

The familiar truths of John 3:16-18 offer this assurance:

For God so loved the world that He gave His only begotten Son, that whoever believes in Him should not perish but have everlasting life. For God did not send His Son into the world to condemn the world, but that the world through Him might be saved. He who believes in Him is not condemned; but he who does not believe is condemned already, because he has not believed in the name of the only begotten Son of God.

Note that the cause of missing salvation is *personal unbelief*, not non-election.

The Lord Jesus had perfect theology regarding these issues and wept over the spiritually resistant people of His day:

"O Jerusalem, Jerusalem, the one who kills the prophets and stones those who are sent to her! How often I wanted to gather your children together, as a hen gathers her chicks under her wings, but you were not willing!" (Matt. 23:37).

This compassion motivates Christ's disciples to serve as His ambassadors: "Now then, we are ambassadors for Christ, as though God were pleading through us: we implore you on Christ's behalf, be reconciled to God" (2 Cor. 5:18-20). The gospel is more than an apparent announcement only valid to those who have been irresistably caused to respond; it is the compelling, compassionate call of our Missionary God.

Although we will never be able to logically reconcile the parallel truths of God's sovereignty and human responsibility, the most practical way to approximate this balance is to consider that believers are elect "according to the foreknowledge of God" in a way that does not exclude anyone from potentially choosing to respond to the loving conviction of the Holy Spirit and to receive Christ as personal Lord and Savior (1 Pet. 1:2).

The LORD guides our lives with mysterious providence, yet offers salvation and assurance to everyone who receives the Lord Jesus. Christ declared:

"Most assuredly, I say to you, he who hears My word and believes in Him who sent Me has everlasting life, and shall not come into judgment, but has passed from death into life" (John 5:24).

6. Insecurity Due to Accusations from the Enemy

If a believer is unsettled in his/her faith and has given ground to the devil, hostile accusations from within can jeopardize his/her sense of security.

Consider this episode from the Old Testament. After Israel returned from the exile of Babylon, the remnant in Canaan faced spiritual warfare from the Enemy. Zechariah chapter four gives a glimpse of a heavenly courtroom where the devil hurled condemnation at Joshua the high priest.[14] This Joshua was a representative of the people of Israel who had been unfaithful to God's covenant:

Then he showed me Joshua the high priest standing before the Angel of the LORD, and Satan standing at his right hand to oppose him. And the LORD said to Satan, "The LORD rebuke you, Satan! The LORD who has chosen Jerusalem rebuke you! Is this not a brand plucked from the fire?" (Zech. 4:1,2).

Thankfully the "Angel [Messenger] of the LORD" was present to serve as an advocate and intercessor for Joshua.

This "Angel" seems to be the pre-incarnate Christ, since the text says "...the LORD said to Satan, 'the LORD rebuke you.'" His redemptive ministry is reaffirmed in 1 John 2:1: "...if anyone sins, we have an Advocate with the Father, Jesus Christ the righteous."

The New Testament also confirms this evil agenda of Satan, who is "the accuser of the brethren" (Rev. 12:11). When the struggling child of God has given ground through lack of surrender to God and/or an area of unbelief, the Enemy exploits this opportunity by firing arrows of accusation (Eph. 4:27; 6:12,16). We are warned by the apostle Paul not to be ignorant of Satan's devices (2 Cor. 2:11).

The dramatic cleansing of Joshua reassures us of the completeness of God's salvation. First, Joshua was cleansed by the removal of his filthy clothing. This symbolizes the removal of sin:

> Now Joshua was clothed with filthy garments, and was standing before the Angel. Then He answered and spoke to those who stood before Him, saying, "Take away the filthy garments from him." And to him He said, "See, I have removed your iniquity from you..." (Zech. 4:3,4).

Second, the high priest was clothed with clean garments, representing the gift of God's righteousness:

> "...and I will clothe you with rich robes." And I said, "Let them put a clean turban on his head." So they put a clean turban on his head, and they put the clothes on him. And the Angel of the LORD stood by (Zech. 4:4b,5).

How wonderful that everyone who repents and places saving faith in the Lord Jesus is totally pardoned (Col. 2:13,14), and receives the gift of God's imputed righteousness! "For He made Him who knew no sin to be sin for us, that we might become the righteousness of God in Him" (2 Cor. 5:21).

Notice in Zechariah's vision that Joshua's efforts were not even addressed; his pardon and justification were solely based on God's amazing grace. As in Joshua's case, your assurance is best affirmed by faith and spiritual growth (Zech. 4:6-10).

So, how can you ward off insecurity that is stirred up by demonic accusation? James gives us concise directions: "Therefore submit to God. Resist the devil and he will flee from you" (James 4:7). Resist him by taking back surrendered ground (Eph. 4:27), and by submission and confession to God. Then lift the "shield of faith" that will deflect the Enemy's lies and deception (Eph. 6:16). As the Lord Jesus quoted strategic Scripture to overcome the devil, likewise you can claim biblical truth and announce the promises of God. Swing the "sword of the Spirit"!

Armed with the victory Christ won at Calvary, appropriate His triumph over the devil's lies. Celebrate your security with the words of the classic hymn, *A Mighty Fortress is Our God*:

> And though this world, with devils filled,
> Should threaten to undo us,
> We will not fear, for God hath willed
> His truth to triumph through us:
> The Prince of Darkness grim,
> we tremble not for him;
> His rage we can endure,
> for lo, his doom is sure,
> One little word shall fell him.[15]

Whether a lack of assurance is caused by one or all six of these roots of insecurity, you can gain confidence in your salvation as you take God at His Word and grow in your relationship with Him.

[8] Loraine Boettner, *The Reformed Doctrine of Pre-destination*, (Presbyterian & Reformed Publishing, 1979), 308. The text usually used to see faith as a direct gift of God is Ephesians 2:8. However, the Greek word for "that" is neuter, whereas *pistis* (faith) is feminine gender. Therefore, the grammar suggests that the gift of God is *salvation by grace through faith.* A. T. Robertson's *Word Pictures in the New Testament.*

[9] For a brief analysis of the five points of Calvinism, see the author's article: *The Sovereignty of God and the Responsibility of Man: A Quest for Balance* at www. GraceNotebook.

For a critique of the view that regeneration occurs prior to personal faith, see Charles Spurgeon's sermon, *The Warrant of Faith*: "If I am to preach faith in Christ to a man who is regenerated, then the man, being regenerated, is saved already, and it is an unnecessary and ridiculous thing for me to preach Christ to him, and bid him to believe in order to be saved when he is saved already, being regenerate. Am I only to preach faith to those who have it? Absurd, indeed! Is not this waiting till the man is cured and then bringing him the medicine? This is preaching Christ to the righteous and not to sinners" (Pasadena, TX: Pilgrim Publications, 1978), p.3]. Quoted in *Reformed Theology and Regeneration*—http://www. middletownbiblechurch.org/reformed/ddregen.htm

[10] Boettner, 309; *Mozley, The Augustinian Doctrine of Predestination*, 45.

[11] Other invitations include Isa. 1:18; 55:1-7; Matt. 22:4; Luke 14:17; Acts 2:21; John 4:14; 7:37,38; Rom. 5:18; 10:9-13; Titus 2:11,12.

[12] Jay Adams, *Competent to Counsel* (Grand Rapids: Baker, 1970), p. 70.

[13] A classic example of this distortion was the rebuke given to pioneer missionary William Carey before he left England for India. The moderator at a ministerial meeting declared: "Young man, sit down. When God decides to save the heathen, He will do it without your help or mine!" J. Herbert Kane, *Christian Missions in Biblical Perspective* (Baker, 1976), 300.

For a scholarly treatment of this complex subject from a foreknowledge perspective, see Norman Geisler, *Chosen but Free: A Balanced View of Divine Election* (Bethany House).

[14] This Joshua is not the successor of Moses named in the book of Joshua (1400 B.C.). The high priest here referred to in the book of Zechariah ministered about 520 B.C. with governor Zerubbabel (Ezra 3:2).

[15] *A Mighty Fortress is Our God*, by Martin Luther (1529); translated from German to English (1853).

Chapter 11
Faith and Good Works

A Study of James 2:14-26

We have a special volunteer at Grace Fellowship International. She has been retired for years, but this has not diminished her commitment to help spread the ministry of Christ-centered counseling. Grace Wilens believes in the value of intercessory prayer. This conviction shows up in her faithful ministry of compiling and sending out the weekly GFI prayer e-mail.[1] Just as Grace's belief in prayer is demonstrated in her prayer letter ministry, so saving faith is revealed in virtuous words and actions. James 2:14-26 shows how *real faith* shows up in a believer's life.

This passage has been a source of confusion to those who think it teaches justification before God by faith *plus* works. When interpreted in context, however, we shall see that the same Holy Spirit who inspired James inspired Paul, who repeatedly taught salvation by grace through faith apart from works. The Holy Spirit does not contradict Himself!

James was warning about the danger of professing faith without really possessing faith. Paul was warning about the danger of trying to add meritorious works to faith as the basis of salvation.[2] Let's explore how James' message unfolds and harmonizes with the rest of the New Testament on this fundamental issue of salvation by grace through faith.

This Scripture introduces the question, "What does it profit, my brethren, if someone says he has faith but does not have works? Can [the] faith save him?" (James 2:14). Notice how the question relates to one's profession: "...if someone says..." It is all too easy to claim belief in Christ without having a saving relationship with Him. How can we differentiate true faith from an imitation? The Greek text reads, "Can the faith [the empty *faith* described in the following examples] save him?" The implied answer is, "No, superficial faith does not save."[3]

James calls attention to the need to demonstrate true faith as an evidence of its reality:

> If a brother or sister is naked and destitute of daily food, and one of you says to them, "Depart in peace, be warmed and filled," but you do not give them the things which are needed for the body, what does it profit? Thus also faith by itself, if it does not have works, is dead (James 2:15-17).

Just saying that the need should be relieved is much different than showing compassion and helping practically.

Commentator Albert Barnes gives the essence of this lesson:

> The individual professes indeed to believe the truths of the gospel; he may be in the church of Christ; he would esteem it a gross calumny to be spoken of as an infidel; but as to any influence which his faith exerts over him, his life would be the same if he had never heard of the gospel. There is not one of the truths of religion which is bodied forth in his life; not a deed to which he is prompted by religion; not an act which could not be accounted for on the supposition that he has no true piety. In such a case, faith may with propriety be said to be dead.[4]

Can real faith be isolated from outward words and actions? An imaginary objector could say: "'You have faith, and I have works.' [James replies] 'Show me your faith without your works, and I will show you my faith by my works.'" Notice again the *show me* emphasis. The only way real faith can be detected by people is if it is manifested in corresponding works.

Mental assent to the reality of God is not enough to bring deliverance from sin and its penalty: "You believe that there is one God. You do well. Even the demons believe—and tremble!" (v.19). Saving faith goes beyond this intellectual agreement; it includes repentance and trust in the Lord Jesus.

Now the great patriarch Abraham is called forward as an example of demonstrated faith:

> Was not Abraham our father justified by works when he offered Isaac his son on the altar? Do you see that faith was working together with his works, and by works faith was made perfect? And the Scripture was fulfilled which says, "Abraham believed God, and it was accounted to him for righteousness." And he was called the friend of God (James 2:21-23).

Notice that Abraham was justified (Gen. 15:6) before he was called upon to dramatically show his faith (Gen. 22:1-19). Abraham was willing to give up Isaac. This was a witness to his servants (Gen. 22:5) and to all who have learned of this famous act of obedience (Heb. 11:17-19).

The conclusion is drawn, "You see then that a man is justified by works, and not by faith only" (James 2:24). Greek scholar A. T. Robertson specified the meaning of "justified" here: "not 'is made righteous,' but 'is shown to be righteous.' James is discussing the proof of faith, not the initial act of being set right with God (Paul's idea in Rom. 4:1-10)."[5]

Not only was Abraham justified by real faith, so was Rahab. Her testimony is also included in the hall of faith: "By faith the harlot Rahab did not perish with those who did not believe, when she had received the spies with peace" (Heb. 11:31). Both the virtuous, male Hebrew and this scarlet lettered, female Gentile were justified by a real faith that was demonstrated practically. James gives this concluding assessment: "For as the body without the spirit is dead, so faith without works is dead also."—i.e., it is lifeless, a mere empty profession.

A key issue in understanding James' argument is the subject. Who "declares righteous" (justifies) the professing believer in this context? Concerning this passage, commentator D. Brown observed,

> To show faith to man, works in some form or other are needed: we are justified judicially by God (Rom. 8:33); meritoriously, by Christ (Isaiah, 53:11); mediately, by faith (Rom. 5:1); evidentially, by works. The question here is not as to the ground on which believers are justified, but about the demonstration of their faith.[6]

So, we see that this passage complements the doctrinal exposition of Paul's epistles (written later):

> Abraham believed God, and it was accounted to him for righteousness." Now to him who works, the wages are not counted as grace but as debt. But to him who does not work but believes on Him who justifies the ungodly, his faith is accounted for righteousness... Therefore we conclude that a man is justified by faith apart from the deeds of the law (Rom. 4:3-5; 3:28).

Faith is the root and good works are the fruit. Christ does the saving: "Who gave Himself for us, that He might redeem us from every lawless deed and purify for Himself

His own special people, zealous for good works" (Titus 2:14).

With justification by faith clarified, don't miss the emphasis of this Scripture. As you abide in Christ, demonstrate your faith through good works!

[1] These e-mails are posted at geewilly.christian-blogsites.com

[2] See Eph. 2:8,9; Gal. 2:16; Rom. 5:1; 10:4

[3] Greek notes: "Rhetorical question..., Condition of third class with *ean* and the present active subjunctive of *legw*, 'if one keep on saying.' ...It is the spurious claim to faith that James here condemns. Can that [the] faith save him? Negative answer expected (*mh*)."—A.T. Robertson, *Word Pictures in the New Testament.*

[4] Albert Barnes, *Notes on the New Testament.*

[5] A. T. Robertson, *Word Pictures in the New Testament.*

[6] Jamieson, Fausset, and Brown, *A Commentary, Critical and Explanatory, on the Old and New Testaments*, 1871. See also on v. 18: "*Show* does not mean here to prove to me, but exhibit to me. Faith is unseen save by God. To show faith to man, works in some form or other are needed..."

Chapter 12
The Unpardonable Sin

A Study of Matthew 12:31,32

A recurring theme in this book is that assurance of salvation is a vital incentive for spiritual growth and fellowship with God. If you are not confident that your name is written in the Book of Life, how can you be secure in depending on Christ moment by moment here and now?

However, one of the issues that has often been a source of confusion and insecurity is that of the *unpardonable sin.* What did Jesus mean by this frightening, solemn warning in Matthew 12:31,32?

> Therefore I say to you, every sin and blasphemy will be forgiven men, but the blasphemy against the Spirit will *not* be forgiven men. Anyone who speaks a word against the Son of Man, it will be forgiven him; but whoever speaks against the Holy Spirit, it will *not* be forgiven him, either in this age or in the age to come.

The author of *Pilgrim's Progress*, John Bunyan, journaled his struggle to gain assurance. This question had troubled him also:

> I had one question that my soul did much desire to be resolved about; and that was, Whether it be possible for any soul that hath indeed sinned the unpar-

donable sin, yet after that to receive though but the least true spiritual comfort from God through Christ? The which, after I had much considered, I found the answer was, No, they could not,...Because they are denied a share in the promise of life; they shall never be forgiven, 'neither in this world, neither in that which is to come' (Matt. 12.32).[1]

This topic has gripped the minds of serious Christians for centuries. Let's examine this passage from Matthew's Gospel in context to clarify the original warning and consider implications for us today. What is the unpardonable sin?

A Miracle with a Message

Matthew 12:22 records an undeniable miracle of the Lord Jesus: "Then one was brought to Him who was demon-possessed, blind and mute; and He healed him, so that the blind and mute man both spoke and saw." The usual practice for an exorcism was to elicit from the demon-possessed person the name of the indwelling demon. However, how could this formula be used when the afflicted person was mute? The promised Messiah was expected to have this kind of unique power and authority. No wonder the witnesses of this deliverance "were amazed and said, 'Could this be the Son of David?'" (Matt. 12:23).

This conclusion was inescapable to the honest, receptive child of Abraham. But how could the Pharisees retain their legalistic traditions and societal prominence when Jesus was authenticating His ministry in this way? They came up with this desperate rationalization: "...they said, 'This fellow does not cast out demons except by Beelzebub, the ruler of the demons'" (Matt. 12:24).

Notice that the miracle was undeniable, but its message was rejected. Christ then demonstrated that their declaration of stubborn unbelief collapses under the weight of its inherent contradictions: 1) Satan casting out his own demons would defeat his own cause by dividing his evil kingdom; 2) Jewish exorcists claimed a success rate in exorcisms, yet they were not accused of operating by Satanic power; 3) Christ's miracle of casting a demon out of a mute, blind man was a convincing evidence that the Kingdom of God had visited them in the person of the King (Matt. 12:25-28).

This is the context of Christ's ominous verdict that the hardened hearts of the religious leaders were beyond the scope of God's forgiveness. Why? Because the Holy Spirit was the source of Christ's miracles (Luke 4:18; John 3:34), and He empowered these signs to confirm the faith of those who were receptive.

The Holy Spirit is the One who draws sinners to the Savior: "... no one speaking by the Spirit of God calls Jesus accursed, and no one can say that Jesus is Lord except by the Holy Spirit" (1 Cor. 12:3). Yet they cursed Jesus by claiming that these miracles were Satanic. This unbelief rejected the implications of Christ's authority over the kingdom of darkness.[2] To blaspheme (blatantly disrespect) the Holy Spirit is to reject the only One who can enable a sinner to repent, believe, and be pardoned.[3]

The Warning for Today

Some propose that this warning about the unpardonable sin doesn't apply after Christ's earthly ministry. After all, Christ is not physically present, doing such miracles as He did in the Gospels. Therefore, the exact circumstances of the unpardonable sin would not be duplicated in this age.

However, the Holy Spirit continues to testify of the person and work of Christ today. In John 16:6-11 Jesus prophesied,

I tell you the truth. It is to your advantage that I go away; for if I do not go away, the Helper will not come to you; but if I depart, I will send Him to you. And when He has come, He will convict the world of sin, and of righteousness, and of judgment: of sin, because they do not believe in Me; of righteousness, because I go to My Father and you see Me no more; of judgment, because the ruler of this world is judged.

The miracles of Christ still speak loudly and clearly from the pages of sacred Scripture. Their purpose is clearly stated: "but these are written that you may believe that Jesus is the Christ, the Son of God, and that believing you may have life in His name" (John 20:31).

So what is the fate of those who reject the convicting work of the Holy Spirit as He testifies through creation, conscience, and Christ? (Rom. 1:16-20; 2:14-16; 5:8). Today, as in the first century, those who die *disbelieving the witness of God's Spirit through the gospel commit the unpardonable sin.*

There will only be two outcomes on the Day of Judgment; to stand in one's own unrighteousness and be condemned, or to stand in Christ's righteousness, having been pardoned. This pardon is available only by grace through repentance and faith. "He who believes in Him [Christ] is not condemned; but he who does not believe is condemned already, because he has not believed in the name of the only begotten Son of God" (John 3:18. See Matt. 25:31-46, Phil. 3:7-9).

An Implicit Consolation

To those who know Christ as their Lord and Savior, Christ's warning has an implicit consolation. All other sins are pardonable. Think of it: No sins are too wicked to be washed away by the precious blood of Christ! (1 Pet. 1:18-20).

Everyone who has heeded the witness of the Holy Spirit's testimony in the gospel has full forgiveness and the basis for unshakable assurance:

> And you, being dead in your trespasses and the uncircumcision of your flesh, He has made alive together with Him, *having forgiven you all trespasses*, having wiped out the handwriting of requirements that was against us, which was contrary to us. And He has taken it out of the way, having nailed it to the cross (Col. 2:13,14).

As the man who was delivered from the demon received his voice and vision, all who believe the witness of the Spirit of God behold His wonders and declare His praise.

[1] John Bunyan (1628-1688), *Grace Abounding to the Chief of Sinners*, par. 220, 221.

[2] Messianic believer, Alfred Edersheim (1825-1889), wrote: "...Once arrived at the conclusion, that the miracles which Christ did were due to the power of Satan, and that He was the representative of the Evil One, their [the leading Pharisees and Sadducees] course was rationally and morally chosen. To regard every fresh manifestation of Christ's Power as only a fuller development of the power of Satan, and to oppose it with increasing determination and hostility, even to the Cross: such was henceforth the natural progress of this history. On the other hand, such a course once fully settled upon, there would, and could, be no further reasoning with, or against it..."—*The Life and Times of Jesus the Messiah*. [Following the text at footnote 2766].

[3] Only God knows when a heart is closed and beyond reach. Such would seem to have been the case with Saul of Tarsus, but the risen Christ apprehended him and made Paul an unparalleled vessel of His grace (Acts 9; Gal. 1:13-17). So, never give up praying for the lost.

Chapter 13
The Cure for Apostasy

A Study of Hebrews 6:1-9

The warning passages in Hebrews 6:1-9 and 10:26-39 are sometimes used to question the security of the believer. We will consider a brief explanation of these passages in their context. This chapter will explore the meaning of the first text:

> Therefore, leaving the discussion of the elementary principles of Christ, let us go on to perfection, not laying again the foundation of repentance from dead works and of faith toward God, of the doctrine of baptisms, of laying on of hands, of resurrection of the dead, and of eternal judgment. And this we will do if God permits. For it is impossible for those who were once enlightened, and have tasted the heavenly gift, and have become partakers of the Holy Spirit, and have tasted the good word of God and the powers of the age to come, if they fall away, to renew them again to repentance, since they crucify again for themselves the Son of God, and put Him to an open shame (Heb. 6:1-6).

This passage has been a challenge to Bible students and space does not allow for an exhaustive treatment of the various grammatical and theological viewpoints. But, the following exposition aims to do justice to the context of this passage and the teaching of the New Testament as a whole.

Let's start with the background. This epistle was written to a predominantly Jewish readership that was being persecuted for their confession of faith in Jesus as the Messiah (Christ). Although the monotheism of the Jews was permitted under Roman law (due to their zeal and heritage) the religion of being Christian was not exempt from the imperial requirement to confess Caesar as Lord. Some who had professed faith in Jesus had returned to the economic, social, legal, and religious safety of Judaism.[1] They were once again looking to the familiar Old Testament rituals as practiced at the Temple in Jerusalem prior to its destruction in A.D. 70.

The author's "word of exhortation" (Heb. 13:22) repeatedly warned these vacillating "converts" about the fatal consequences of looking away from Christ for another means of salvation.

> How shall we escape if we neglect so great a salvation, which at the first began to be spoken by the Lord, and was confirmed to us by those who heard Him, God also bearing witness both with signs and wonders, with various miracles, and gifts of the Holy Spirit, according to His own will? (Heb. 2:3,4).

Leading up to chapter six is a section that rebukes the congregation for their lack of learning and neglect of spiritual growth:

> For though by this time you ought to be teachers, you need someone to teach you again the first principles of the oracles of God; and you have come to need milk and not solid food. For everyone who partakes only of milk is unskilled in the word of righteousness, for he is a babe. But solid food belongs to those who are of full age, that is, those who by reason of

use have their senses exercised to discern both good and evil (Heb. 5:12-14).

The best way to gain confidence in the faith is to learn; the best way to demonstrate life is to grow.

The writer urges, "Therefore, leaving the discussion of the elementary principles of Christ, let us go on to perfection" [i.e., maturity—Col. 1:28; 4:12]. The teaching about Christ's high priestly ministry in chapters 7-10 would be like solid food in comparison to milk. Therefore, the basic "milk" teachings would not be reviewed at this juncture (Heb. 6:1,2).

Another reason for going on to a more comprehensive understanding of Christ's superiority to the Old Covenant priesthood was that these basics would not be adequate to restore a backslidden believer. (By "backslidden" I refer to professing believers who had returned to confidence in the Temple rituals or were tempted to do so). Such a turning away from Christ is known as *apostasy* (2 Pet. 2:20-22).

Scholars debate whether the scenario of Hebrews 6:4,5 refers to those who were almost saved and then fell away *or* to those who were truly born again but (actually or hypothetically) lost their salvation. This passage has been difficult for both Calvinistic and Arminian viewpoints. It is difficult for Calvinists because it sounds like the saved person falls away and does not persevere. It is difficult for Arminians because those who "fall away" cannot be renewed to repentance (Heb. 6:6).

Space precludes a discussion of those viewpoints. However, let's take a closer look at verse 6: "...if they fall away, [it is impossible] to renew them again to repentance, since they crucify again for themselves the Son of God, and put Him to an open shame" (Heb. 6:6).

Translations seem to present a *reason* apostates cannot be restored to repentance: "since they crucify again for themselves the Son of God..." However, consider the phrase as describing the *condition* of those who were temporarily enticed back to Temple worship. Those returning to Judaism were avoiding persecution, but thereby insinuating that the animal sacrifices were still necessary for atonement, even after Christ's perfect sacrifice on Calvary. This would be "putting Him to an open shame." I believe that a closer look at the grammar substantiates this view.

"Since" (Heb. 6:6) is not in the original text; rather, it is supplied to complement the verb "crucify again." This verb is a present, active participle, conveying the idea that they were in a condition of desecrating Christ's sacrifice (by preferring temple sacrifices). So the text should read, "it is impossible to renew them again to repentance *while they* crucify again for themselves the Son of God...."

What is the remedy for this wavering confession of faith that is inclined to take refuge in Judaism? The remedy is to go on to the deeper truths of Christ's Superior priesthood! Thus, these backsliders *could be restored to repentance if they were persuaded by the more complete revelation of God's Word.* And this fits the progression of thought in Hebrews 7:1-10:24.

The author is warning the readers as a pastor, not speculating about their ultimate decisions. The doctrinal debate about the possibility or impossibility of losing one's salvation is not directly addressed here. However, saving faith is described as a faith that continues to believe (Heb. 3:6; Col. 1:23; 1 Cor. 15:2).

This warning is then illustrated from nature:

For the earth which drinks in the rain that often comes upon it, and bears herbs useful for those by whom it is cultivated, receives blessing from God; but if it bears thorns and briars, it is rejected and near to being cursed [the backsliders were flirting with judgment], whose end is to be burned (Heb. 6:7,8).

After this warning and an explanation of his strategy to present the supremacy and finality of Christ's person and work, the author reassures the Hebrew recipients of this letter that he expects them to persevere: "But, beloved, we are confident of better things concerning you, yes, things that accompany salvation, though we speak in this manner" (Heb. 6:9).

In the next chapter we'll study a parallel passage with a similar theme. Therefore, don't fear that true faith in Christ is not adequate to keep you securely in Christ. This book also assures us, "This hope we have as an anchor of the soul, both sure and steadfast, and which enters the Presence behind the veil" (Heb. 6:19). So, gain confidence in your faith by digesting the meat of the Word. Demonstrate your spiritual life by growth.

[1] In addition to Roman oppression there was resistance from Jewish society: "The numerous Christian churches scattered throughout Judaea (Ac 9:31; Ga 1:22) were continually exposed to persecution from the Jews (1 Thess. 2:14), which would become more searching and extensive as churches multiplied, and as the growing turbulence of the nation ripened into the insurrection of A. D. 66. Personal violence, spoliation of property, exclusion from the synagogue, and domestic strife were the universal forms of persecution. But in Jerusalem there was one additional weapon in the hands of the predominant oppressors of the Christians. Their magnificent national Temple, hallowed to every Jew by ancient historical and by gentler personal recollections, with its irresistible attractions, its soothing strains, and mysterious ceremonies, might be shut against the Hebrew Christian."—*Smith Bible Dictionary*, "The Epistle to the Hebrews."

Chapter 14
No Alternatives

A Study of Hebrews 10:26-31

The parallel warning passage to Hebrews 6:1-9 gives a similar, strong message. Hebrews 10:26-31 has caused many believers to question their salvation: "For *if we sin willfully* after we have received the knowledge of the truth, there no longer remains a sacrifice for sins" (Heb. 10:26). Does this mean that an intentional sin in a Christian's life is unforgivable? Although the Old Testament made a distinction concerning defiant, high-handed sins, the New Testament depiction of sins assumes identifiable acts of commission or omission. These are basically willful, since they are chosen courses of actions, words, and attitudes. However, Colossians 2:13 assures the true believer of complete forgiveness: "And you, being dead in your trespasses and the uncircumcision of your flesh, He has made alive together with Him, *having forgiven you all trespasses.*" There is no limitation of pardon and cleansing to unintentional sins.

To understand the warning in this chapter, then, we need to first look at the preceding context. Hebrews 10:1-18 explains the perfect, complete sacrifice that Christ made on Calvary. This is followed by exhortations to live in light of this full salvation (Heb. 10:19-24). The concluding admonition involves the importance of Christian fellowship:

And let us consider one another in order to stir up love and good works, not forsaking the assembling

103

of ourselves together, as is the manner of some, but exhorting one an-other, and so much the more as you see the Day approaching (Heb. 10:24,25).

Now comes the strong warning:

For if we sin willfully after we have received the knowledge of the truth, there no longer remains a sacrifice for sins, but a certain fearful expectation of judgment, and fiery indignation which will devour the adversaries (Heb. 10:26,27).

The question is, What is meant by the willful sin in verse 26? To answer this we need to observe that the context is describing the superiority and finality of Christ's New Covenant. The issue of "sin willfully" does not refer to any or all intentional sins. *This willful sin refers to the intentional rejection of the New Covenant in Christ Jesus.*[1]

Dire consequences of judgment are given to warn the wavering person to escape such a dreadful destiny. The following verses confirm this warning by comparing the sin of apostasy from Christ to that of apostasy from the Old Covenant under Moses: "Anyone who has rejected Moses' law dies without mercy on the testimony of two or three witnesses" (Heb. 10:28). Cases of idolatry (Deut. 17:2-7) and high-handed rejection of God's authority (Num. 15:30,31) deserves capital punishment.

The next verse shows that rejecting the New Covenant in Christ is even more blameworthy: "Of how much worse punishment, do you suppose, will he be thought worthy who has trampled the Son of God underfoot...." The one who turns his back on Christ treats the Atonement with contempt. He has "counted the blood of the covenant by which he was sanctified a common thing." Although Christ's payment for sin is sufficient for all (1 John 2:2), rejecting the gospel insinuates that Christ's sacrifice was no better than that of an animal or martyr.

This stubborn unbelief has "insulted the Spirit of grace" (Heb. 10:29), since the Spirit of God convicts people of their need and the truth of the gospel (John 16:8-11; 1 Cor. 12:3).

The danger of a professing Christian forsaking Christ brings this additional warning:

> For we know Him who said, "Vengeance is Mine, I will repay," says the Lord. And again, "The LORD will judge His people." It is a fearful thing to fall into the hands of the living God (Heb. 10:30,31; Deut. 32:35,36).[2]

This "hell fire and brimstone" language may seem harsh, but God's love is perfectly balanced by His justice (Rom. 3:26).

The next verses would reassure the persecuted Jewish believers in the early church:

> But recall the former days in which, after you were illuminated, you endured a great struggle with sufferings: partly while you were made a spectacle both by reproaches and tribulations, and partly while you became companions of those who were so treated; for you had compassion on me in my chains, and joyfully accepted the plundering of your goods, knowing that you have a better and an enduring possession for yourselves in heaven. Therefore do not cast away your confidence, which has great reward. For you have need of endurance, so that after you have done the will of God, you may receive the [fulfillment of the] promise (Heb. 10:32-36).

To ears of Christians in the Western World, it is difficult to comprehend this kind of suffering for Christ, yet even today thousands of believers are experiencing persecution around the world.[3]

The author of Hebrews concludes this section with a quote from Habakkuk. This Old Testament prophet had addressed the importance of being part of the faithful remnant in the days of foreign oppression: "For yet a little while, And He who is coming will come and will not tarry. Now the just shall live by faith; But if anyone draws back, My soul has no pleasure in him" (Heb. 10:37,38; Hab. 2:3,4).[4] As the believers in the days of Habakkuk anticipated God delivering them from Babylon, so New Covenant believers anticipate Christ's return (Titus 2:13,14). The mention of not "drawing back" warns professing Christians to not turn away from Christ in resolute unbelief. However, the passage ends with a word of assurance: "But we are not of those who draw back to perdition, but of those who believe to the saving of the soul" (Heb. 10:39).

This study has concluded that: 1) True believers will continue to believe in Christ (Heb. 3:7); 2) The willful sin here is not an act of disobedience or a condition of temporary backsliding.[5] The willful sin is an unrepentant turning away from Christ's New Covenant.[6]

In Hebrews, chapter 6, the cure for apostasy is to learn and believe the meat of the Word—the New Testament truth of Christ's superior, high priestly ministry. The warning in chapter 10 is to continue in the privileges of New Covenant faith and fellowship. If an inquirer turns away from Christ's once-for-all atonement, there are no sacrifices that could redeem a person and qualify him/her for heaven.

Ultimately our confidence is in the One who saves completely: "Therefore He is also able to save to the uttermost those who come to God through Him, since He always lives to make intercession for them" (Heb. 7:25). You can count on your Redeemer's faithfulness! "For He Himself has said, 'I will never leave you nor forsake you'" (Heb. 13:5).

[1] "Sin" is a present active participle in Greek, indicating a condition. "*Sin* here means, ...apostasize (Heb. 3:12) to Judaism or infidelity, [it] is not a sin of ignorance, or error...[or] of infirmity, but a deliberate sinning against the Spirit (Heb. 10:29 Heb. 5:2) ...a sinning presumptuously and perseveringly against Christ's redemption for us, and the Spirit of grace in us." Jamieson, Fausset, and Brown, *Commentary on the Whole Bible.*

[2] "The idea here is, that to fall into the hands of the Lord [2 Sam. 24], after having despised his mercy and rejected his salvation, would be [terrifying]; and the fear of this should deter from the commission of the dreadful crime. The phrase *living God* is used in the Scripture in opposition to idols. God always lives; his power is capable of being always exerted." Albert Barnes, *Notes on the New Testament.*

[3] For example, see Voice of the Martyrs: www.Persecution.org

[4] "But if anyone draws back, My soul has no pleasure in him" is based on the Greek translation of the Old Testament (LXX) commonly used in the first century.

[5] God can and will discipline and restore His erring children:

"My son, do not despise the chastening of the LORD,
Nor be discouraged when you are rebuked by Him;
For whom the LORD loves He chastens,
And scourges every son whom He receives"
(Heb. 12:5,6).

[6] Whether one believes that a born again Christian cannot lose his/her salvation or can intentionally forfeit it, God's Word warns everyone in the strongest possible

terms that there is no other way of redemption, forgiveness, and salvation except through faith in Jesus the Messiah.

Chapter 15
Broken Branches

A Study of Romans 11:17-23

One of the vivid metaphors of the believer's union with Christ is that of a grafted branch. The Lord Jesus uses this image extensively in John 15:1-8 where He is the true vine and believers are branches.

In verse two Christ declared, "Every branch in Me that does not bear fruit He takes away" (John 15:2a). This statement has raised questions in many who wonder, "If I lack fruit will I be "taken away" and lose my salvation?" *Takes away* is based on the Greek term *airo*, which essentially means: "to raise up, elevate, lift up."[1] The ones who temporarily are unfruitful are "lifted up" through cleansing, support, and positioning in the sun. Those temporarily unfruitful should not be confused with the branches mentioned in verse six. The ones who profess belief without a personal relationship with Christ are the lifeless branches that are collected and burned (John 15:6).

A similar comparison is used in Romans 11:16-26. Here believing Israel is symbolized by an olive tree. In the context, the apostle Paul is defending the faithfulness, sovereignty, and wisdom of God. Although God had chosen Israel as His covenant people and promised them the Messiah, their leaders had rejected the Lord Jesus. Let's delve into this passage further.

To understand this apparent inconsistency in the purposes of the LORD, we need His wisdom. Paul gave a preliminary defense of God's wisdom in 1 Corinthians 2:7,8:

But we speak the wisdom of God in a mystery, the hidden wisdom which God ordained before the ages for our glory, which none of the rulers of this age knew; for had they known, they would not have crucified the Lord of glory.

In Romans chapter 11, those Israelites who have rejected Messiah Jesus have forfeited their privileges and salvation as God's chosen people. As such, they are represented by the natural branches that are broken off from the olive tree of redemption (v.17; John 19:17; Acts 2:23; 3:14-20). The apostle Peter had boldly proclaimed to the nation's leaders,

Let it be known to you all, and to all the people of Israel, that by the name of Jesus Christ of Nazareth, whom you crucified, whom God raised from the dead, by Him this man [supernaturally healed] stands here before you whole. This is the stone which was rejected by you builders, which has become the chief cornerstone. Nor is there salvation in any other, for there is no other name under heaven given among men by which we must be saved (Acts 4:10-12).

The gospel still has a special priority to those with a Jewish heritage: "For I am not ashamed of the gospel of Christ, for it is the power of God to salvation for everyone who believes, for the Jew first and also for the Greek" (Rom. 1:16). Nevertheless, the apostasy of the Israelite leaders before governor Pilate, steered the descendants of Abraham, Isaac, Jacob, and David on a detour from God's redemptive purpose. Paul elsewhere described this reluctance to believe in Messiah Jesus as a "veil" over their hearts (2 Cor. 3:14-16).

Returning to the metaphor of the olive tree, the Gentiles who come to saving faith in Messiah (Christ) are like branches that are grafted into this olive tree of redemption:

> Some of the branches were broken off, and you [Gentile believers], being a wild olive tree, were grafted in among them, and with them became a partaker of the root and fatness of the olive tree... (Rom. 11:17a).

How wonderful is God's grace! He includes those who traditionally had been strangers to His covenants of promise (Eph. 2:12,13). The Holy Spirit has also revealed that Jew and Gentile believers now form one organic family of faith—the dwelling place of God, the Body of Christ (Eph. 2:14-22;1:23; Gal. 3:26-28).

Now the apostle warns Gentile Christians to avoid a smug, self-righteous disdain for Jewish unbelievers. Rather, they should have a reverent gratitude for God's condescending grace:

> Do not boast against the branches [the Jewish people]. But if you do boast, remember that you do not support the root, but the root [the Jewish heritage of faith] supports you. You will say then, "Branches were broken off that I might be grafted in" (Rom. 11:17b-19).

A further warning is given to the church. If Israel could take for granted their privileged position and miss the blessings of the new covenant, the professing Christian church faces this same risk! Salvation is based on personal saving faith; it is not bestowed upon church members by virtue of worship attendance, baptism, creed, or tradition. Paul continued,

> Because of unbelief they [Jewish unbelievers] were broken off, and you stand by faith. Do not be haughty, but fear. For if God did not spare the natural

branches, He may not spare you either. Therefore consider the goodness and severity of God: on those who fell, severity; but toward you, goodness, if you continue in His goodness. Otherwise you also will be cut off (Rom. 11:20-22).

Notice the context of this warning. Some have mistakenly assumed that an individual, regenerated child of God could be "cut off" and lose his/her salvation. In response, observe that:

1) Those who are regenerated will continue to believe as a sign of their genuine faith and the presence of the Holy Spirit (Col. 1:23; Heb. 3:6; Eph. 4:30);

2) Paul's warning is *not* addressed to an individual, but the corporate, Gentile professing church.

Church history bears sad testimony to the validity of this warning. For example, the churches addressed by the resurrected Christ in Revelation 2:1-3:20 have had their testimony snuffed out under the march of Islam. A church can drift away from the essentials of biblical truth and cease communicating the gospel. Or, an explicitly false gospel may replace the true one, so the hearers become just as deceived as those who intentionally disassociate themselves from Christ Jesus (Gal. 1:8,9).

Such apostasy among supposed Christian churches will increase in the last days: "Now the Spirit expressly says that in latter times some will depart from the faith, giving heed to deceiving spirits and doctrines of demons" (1 Tim. 4:1). This has been fulfilled in our generation by liberal, Bible-denying churches and the cults. This trend was symbolized to me on a visit to Toronto, Canada. I drove by a stately, aged church building and did a double-take. Instead of the expected Christian sign on the front, two large sings proclaimed the identity of its new tenants: "HARE KRISHNA."

Just as Paul's defense in Romans 9-11 concerns God's faithfulness to Israel as a people, so the warning about ceasing to believe is aimed at the Gentile church. This caution is echoed in the epistle of Jude. He wrote,

> Beloved, while I was very diligent to write to you concerning our common salvation, I found it necessary to write to you exhorting you to contend earnestly for the faith which was once for all delivered to the saints. For certain men have crept in unnoticed, who long ago were marked out for this condemnation, ungodly men, who turn the grace of our God into lewdness and deny the only Lord God and our Lord Jesus Christ (Jude 1:3,4).

May this admonition garrison the hearts of church leaders that they would be faithful to the inerrant, infallible Word of God (2 Tim. 3:16).

Jude concludes his letter with a fitting promise to those who have received Christ as Lord and Savior:

> Now to Him who is able to keep you from stumbling,
> And to present you faultless
> Before the presence of His glory with exceeding joy,
> To God our Savior, Who alone is wise,
> Be glory and majesty, Dominion and power,
> Both now and forever. Amen (vv. 24,25).

[1] *Thayers Greek Lexicon.* Bruce Wilkinson also brings out this clarification on John 15:2 in *Secrets of the Vine* (Sisters, OR: Multnomah, 2001).

Chapter 16
Rebukes in Revelation

A Study of Revelation 2:1-3:21

In Chapters two and three of the Revelation, the risen Christ sent messages through the apostle John to seven churches of the first century. These were representative congregations of professed believers. Their locations and the sequence of the short letters follow a clockwise circuit in Asia Minor beginning at Ephesus and concluding at Laodicea.

The stern tone of parts of these epistles may unsettle an insecure believer. "Is the Lord mad at me? Will I be punished or cast out? What does it mean to overcome?"

The seven letters follow a basic pattern: 1) a pictographic description of the risen Christ, 2) commendation of their good works, 3) a rebuke for areas of unfaithfulness, 4) admonitions to correct the church, and 5) promises to overcomers. Smyrna and Philadelphia churches were not rebuked; suffering and perseverance evidently kept their priorities straight. Consider some issues in Revelation 2:1-3:20 that relate to assurance and security.

Who Are the Overcomers?

At first glance the promises to overcomers seem to be addressed to a special class of Christians—those who end their lives triumphantly: "He who has an ear, let him hear what the Spirit says to the churches. To him who overcomes I will give to eat from the tree of life, which is in the midst of the Paradise of God" (Rev. 2:7,11,17,26; 3:5,12,21). In a sense this is true, since every born again believer is "kept by the power of God through faith for salvation ready to be revealed in the last time" (1 Peter 1:5). Ultimate salvation is always a victory over death and judgment. The human author of Revelation defined the "overcomer" in an earlier epistle: "For whatever is born of God overcomes the world. And this is the victory that has overcome the world—our faith. Who is he who overcomes the world, but he who believes that Jesus is the Son of God?" (1 John 5:4,5). In this sense every regenerate believer is descibed as an overcomer. Continued faith is the essence of victory (Col.1:23).

Regrettably, not all heaven-bound believers finish their race victoriously, even though that is the goal and desire of every true Christian. Some will miss out on their potential and rewards like Demas evidently did. For a good while he was a trusted ministry associate of the apostle Paul, but later he got off track: "for Demas has forsaken me, having loved this present world, and has departed for Thessalonica...." (2 Tim. 4:10). How different he was from Paul, who was committed to finishing the Christian race well. He did not want to lose any potential rewards or discredit the Savior. Paul confided in the Corinthians,

> Therefore I run thus: not with uncertainty. Thus I fight: not as one who beats the air. But I discipline my body and bring it into subjection, lest, when I have preached to others, I myself should become disqualified [for the prize] (1 Cor. 9:26,27; see Phil 3:14; 2 Cor 5:10).

No wonder Paul could testify before his martyrdom,

> I have fought the good fight, I have finished the race, I have kept the faith. Finally, there is laid up for me

the crown of righteousness, which the Lord, the righteous Judge, will give to me on that Day, and not to me only but also to all who have loved His appearing (2 Tim. 4:7,8).

Will Uncommitted Believers Be Rejected?

The tone of rebuke in five of these letters reflects God's righteousness and holiness. The churches were to have testimonies that shone brightly in a pagan culture. Therefore, any doctrinal, moral, or spiritual problems were serious concerns. Rebuke and correction are essential qualities of God's Word (2 Tim. 3:16). These issues deserved the Lord's censure: a lack of love for Christ (Ephesus), toleration of immorality and idolatry (Pergamos and Thyatira), heresy (Pergamos), and lukewarmness (Laodicea).

The warnings involved underscored exhortations to repentance and obedience. The Lord reassured them that love was motivating this discipline (Rev. 3:19). The consequences of continued error was the potential loss of their corporate witness: "Remember therefore from where you have fallen; repent and do the first works, or else I will come to you quickly and remove your lampstand from its place..." (Rev. 2:5). How sad it is when a church's light dims and goes out. Centuries later this happened to Asia Minor's historic churches through their subjugation by Islam.

A text which some have interpreted as teaching insecurity is the warning to the Laodiceans in Revelation 3:16: "So then, because you are lukewarm, and neither cold nor hot, I will vomit you out of My mouth." This strong, eastern figure of speech is related to the metaphors in this letter. Christ spoke of the alternatives of water being hot or cold. The church's condition was "lukewarm."

"Hot" seems to refer to a faithful commitment to the truth of the gospel accompanied by a zealous, faithful commitment to the Lord. The "hot" water was probably an allusion to the medicinal hot springs of nearby Hieropolis. "Lukewarm" was the unpleasant state of being in between hot and cold. It may have alluded to the water that was supplied to Laodicea by a long set of pipes, rendering the water almost undrinkable. What, then, did "cold" symbolize here? Usually this "cold" option has been viewed as referring to an unsaved, unbelieving condition. If so, why would Christ prefer the cold state to believers being lukewarm? Surely, the Lord is not saying He would rather have an individual die as a lost person, rather than being a fully devoted disciple! That would be totally out of character with His redeeming love and His awareness of human struggles (John 15:13; Heb. 4:14-16).

In this context Christ is speaking of their corporate witness, not an individual's standing before God (which is based on grace—Rom. 5:1-4). If "cold" refers to a person who has not professed faith in Christ, how would this be preferable to being lukewarm? Pastor Albert Barnes lists several reasons that would justify this conclusion. For example, a known unbeliever would be more reachable, since he has not identified with the church; his need of the gospel is obvious to Christians. However self-righteousness (a lukewarm condition) would hinder one's true conversion (Matt. 7:21-23). A person needs to confess his lost condition in order to be "found" (Luke 15:1-31). Concerning his witness to others, the unbeliever avoids the hypocrisy of saying one thing but believing and living in a contradictory way. This lukewarm condition is a stumbling block to outsiders.[1]

Another possible interpretation of "cold" is that it symbolizes a quality of refreshing fellow believers. In this case Christ prefers "cold" to lukewarmness, which fails to refresh while also failing to be hot. Hot (medicinal waters) would symbolize a radiant, prophetic witness to a secular world.

This use of "cold" may allude to the cold mountain streams of Colosse.[2] Paul affirmed a church leader in Colosse named Philemon who had a reputation for refreshing encouragement for those who came to his house church: "For we have great joy and consolation in your love, because the hearts of the saints have been refreshed by you, brother" (Phile. 7).

These seven letters prompted the churches of Asia Minor to individual faithfulness and collective effectiveness. In this way they would be strategic outposts of the kingdom of God in Roman culture. The warnings in these epistles need to be balanced with God's promises never to cast out His redeemed ones. Christ assures His people,

> All that the Father gives Me will come to Me, and the one who comes to Me I will by no means cast out... This is the will of the Father who sent Me, that of all He has given Me I should lose nothing, but should raise it up at the last day (John 6:37,39).

All seven letters conclude with symbolic expressions of rewards that await the people of God. For example, Revelation 3:12 states:

> He who overcomes, I will make him a pillar in the temple of My God [security and access], and he shall go out no more [permanence]. And I will write on him the name of My God and the name of the city of My God, the New Jerusalem, which comes down out of heaven from My God. And I will write on him My new name [identity and glory].

Reassured by His grace, demonstrate your loyalty to your risen, glorified Savior. Renounce fleshly inconsistencies, and yield to the indwelling Holy Spirit. Let your light shine, as you anticipate your glorious heavenly welcome!

[1] Albert Barnes, *Notes on the New Testament.*

[2] The historical allusions to Hierapolis and Colosse are documented in the notes of The Geneva Study Bible at Revelation 3:15. The interpretation of "cold" water as refreshing is in The Nelson Study Bible notes at Revelation 3:16.

Blessed Reassurance

Chapter 17
Fallen into Legalism

A Study of Galatians 5:3-6

Some major airports have installed a system that helps passengers who must walk long distances in the concourses. The moving walkway (or moving sidewalk) functions like an escalator, but transports people horizontally instead of at an incline. Passengers can stand or walk as this conveyor belt walkway carries them forward. I've enjoyed using them in Atlanta, Miami, and elsewhere. Caution is needed as you enter and eventually exit this system. A recording is heard near the end of the path that warns the passengers to avoid tripping as they exit the moving walkway.

Speed-enhanced movement on such a moving walkway is obviously superior to walking in your own strength (unless your goal is exercise!). Similarly, the walk of Christians is greatly enhanced when they are carried along by God's grace and Spirit.

Paul was gripped by the dangerous situation in Galatia when the church was being tempted to turn away from a super-natural walk. They were being exposed to false teachers—the Judaizers—who were trying to persuade them that Christians had to add the law of Moses to the gospel in order to be saved and sanctified. Notice the apostle's intense warning about defending the gospel of grace: "But even if we, or an angel from heaven, preach any other gospel to you than what we have preached to you, let him be accursed" (Gal. 1:8). Galatians goes on to defend the revelation of the gospel, clarify the role of the law, and vindicate the need for Spirit-filled, grace-oriented discipleship.

The way of salvation is by grace through faith, apart from any meritorious works. Paul declared:

> Knowing that a man is not justified by the works of the law but by faith in Jesus Christ, even we have believed in Christ Jesus, that we might be justified by faith in Christ and not by the works of the law; for by the works of the law no flesh shall be justified (Gal. 2:16).

The law of Moses was never intended to bring salvation. Rather, it revealed the nature of sin as the transgression of God's holy standards. In turn, the law system was to lead the condemned sinner to the only One who could grant pardon and spiritual life: "Therefore the law was our tutor to bring us to Christ, that we might be justified by faith. But after faith has come, we are no longer under a tutor" (Gal. 3:24,25).

Notice how the Galatian believers had been misled by the legalists:

> O foolish Galatians! Who has bewitched you that you should not obey the truth, before whose eyes Jesus Christ was clearly portrayed among you as crucified? This only I want to learn from you: Did you receive the Spirit by the works of the law, or by the hearing of faith? Are you so foolish? Having begun in the Spirit, are you now being made perfect by the flesh? (Gal. 3:1-3).

So, not only was the good news of grace essential for salvation; it was also essential for Christian living. The believers were warned accordingly: "Stand fast therefore in the liberty by which Christ has made us free, and do not be entangled again with a yoke of bondage" (Gal. 5:1). The sacrificial laws were superseded by the finality of Christ's one-for-all sacrifice at Calvary (Heb. 10:8-14). The civil and dietary laws were also done away with when God created the spiritual organism of the church as equally Jew and Gentile (Eph. 2:14-22; Col 2:16-17).

In this context, a further caution is mentioned, since some were reverting to a hybrid of Judaism and Jesus:

> "And I testify again to every man who becomes circumcised [subjecting himself to that operation to become Jewish in order to become right with God] that he is a debtor to keep the whole law. You have become estranged from Christ, you who attempt to be justified by law; you have fallen from grace" (Gal. 5:3,4).

The phrase, "fallen from grace," has been interpreted to mean "fallen from salvation." Even though grace is essential to salvation, notice that the context is the deceptive influence of legalism. If "grace" is undeserved kindness, how could it require performance to retain it? Notice the clarity of Scripture concerning grace apart from works: "But to him who does not work but believes on Him who justifies the ungodly, his faith is accounted for righteousness" (Rom. 4:5).

What, then, is the meaning of this warning to not fall from grace? The issue is what erring believers would fall into if they fell from grace. *They would not fall into damnation, but into legalism.* The next verses demonstrate the importance of God's Spirit and grace in salvation and sanctification: "For we through the Spirit eagerly wait for the hope of righteousness by faith [not a mixture of law]. For in Christ Jesus neither circumcision nor uncircumcision avails anything, but *faith* working through love" (Gal. 5:5,6).

By "uncircumcision" here, the apostle is saying that virtue does not come by being non-Jewish either. Eternal and abundant life comes by grace through faith in Christ alone! "For in Christ Jesus neither circumcision nor uncircumcision avails anything, but a new creation" (Gal. 6:15).

We lapse into legalism if we live in fear of condemnation, work for God in an effort to deserve His acceptance, focus on external, man-made standards, or try to walk as a Christian in our own strength.

In case the pendulum should swing to the opposite extreme, Paul goes on to clarify, "For you, brethren, have been called to liberty; only do not use liberty as an opportunity for the flesh, but through love serve one another" (Gal. 5:13). Instead of living according to the old, worldly patterns, believers need to walk in the power and control of the Holy Spirit: "I say then: Walk in the Spirit, and you shall not fulfill the lust of the flesh" (Gal. 5:16).

Just as the moving walkway broadcasts a warning for passengers not to stumble into unassisted walking, so the disciple of Christ is cautioned not to stumble into legalistic self-effort.

Paul testified about the secret of moving ahead in the spiritual, grace walk:

I have been crucified with Christ; it is no longer I who live, but Christ lives in me; and the life which I now live in the flesh I live by faith in the Son of God, who loved me and gave Himself for me (Gal. 2:20).

May the fullness of the gospel enable you to walk supernaturally in the power of the Holy Spirit.

Chapter 18
The Futility of False Teaching

In his book, *The Case for Faith*, Lee Strobel interviewed a prominent skeptic named Charles Templeton. The one being interviewed had a sad tone. This elderly religious author was reflecting on his early years as an evangelist. At that time, some considered him a better preacher than Billy Graham. Yet, eventually, Templeton renounced the gospel he had formerly preached. Strobel probed the issues of his unbelief, their causes, and consequences.[1] This leads to some searching questions: Did the former evangelist loose his salvation? How could he have preached the gospel to others, then personally rejected Jesus Christ?

In cases such as this—whether in the news or in our own network of acquaintances—we are prone to assume that we know a person's heart. Scripture reminds us, however, that "man looks at the outward appearance, but the LORD looks at the heart" (1 Sam. 16:7b). We cannot say with finality whether such persons ever had saving faith, or if they had head knowledge of the Savior and later changed their mind. In another case, a person may be regenerate, yet in a backslidden condition. We then expect God's chastisement to be administered, although we may not perceive how that is happening. Yet the Holy Spirit will be convicting them. As God declared to wayward Judah, "'Return, O backsliding children,' says the LORD; 'for I am married to you. I will take you, one from a city and two from a family, and I will bring you to Zion'" (Jer. 3:14). In wresting with the issues of assurance and security, we face a temptation to interpret the Bible ac-

127

cording to our circumstances and experiences. However, God summons us to do the opposite: interpret your experiences (and those of others) in the light of God's Word.

These concerns about professing disciples who revert to unbelief are dealt with in 2 Peter chapter two. Verse one launches into a warning:

> "But there were also false prophets among the people, even as there will be false teachers among you, who will secretly bring in destructive heresies, even denying the Lord who bought them, and bring on themselves swift destruction."

These false teachers would be especially dangerous because of their former agreement with Christianity. The text mentions that they denied "the Lord who bought them." Usually this would imply that the persons described had savingly believed on Christ. However, the Scriptures also affirm that Christ's payment on Calvary was sufficient for all people—even those who are never reconciled to God. As Hebrews 2:9 puts it,

> "But we see Jesus, who was made a little lower than the angels, for the suffering of death crowned with glory and honor, that He, by the grace of God, *might taste death for everyone*" (Cf. 1 John 2:2).

Therefore, the false teachers had a former interest in the sacrifice of Christ on the cross, but were not personally redeemed.

This chapter has been outlined as follows:

1. The danger of false teachers (2:1-3),
2. The destruction of false teachers (2:4-9), and
3. The description of false teachers (2:10-22).[2]

As we consider the characteristics of these false teachers, their traits show their counterfeit spirituality. They act like "brute beasts" (carnal), like "spots and blemishes" corrupting the Christians' communal meals, and—like the prophet Balaam—they opt for an alternate message that will increase their financial gain. A dreadful punishment awaits them: "These are wells without water, clouds carried by a tempest, for whom is reserved the blackness of darkness forever" (2 Pet. 2:17).

With this context in mind, we come to a passage that has sometimes been interpreted as teaching insecurity:

> "For if, after they have escaped the pollutions of the world through the knowledge of the Lord and Savior Jesus Christ, they are again entangled in them and overcome, the latter end is worse for them than the beginning" (2 Pet. 2:20).

The false teachers experienced an outer reformation, appearing as tares among the wheat (Matt. 13:25-30). Their latter end of unbelief is worse because of the light that they have rejected. One of the factors that will determine the degree of eternal punishment of the lost is the amount of opportunity and spiritual light they suppressed and rejected (Luke 12:47,48; Matt. 11:20-24). The apostate teachers had learned about scriptural truth, then turned their back on it.

The next verse confirms this indictment:

> "For it would have been better for them not to have known the way of righteousness, than having known it, to turn from the holy commandment delivered to them" (2 Pet. 2:21).

Notice that they turn from the holy commandment (the Lord's gospel) not the Lord Himself (since they had not truly turned to Him in the first place).

The following comparisons confirm this conclusion:

"But it has happened to them according to the true proverb: 'A dog returns to his own vomit,' and, 'a sow, having washed, to her wallowing in the mire'" (2 Pet. 2:22).

This behavior of meandering dogs would be familiar to the middle eastern readers. The false prophets had been self-centered and sensual; they temporarily reformed, then returned to their natural, evil ways. A pig may be washed and perfumed, but its natural habitat is the muddy pen; its return shows its "porky" nature! By way of contrast, true believers are portrayed as sheep, not unclean pigs. Peter does not describe a pig that becomes a lamb, then later becomes a pig again. Rather, the pig is cleaned up, then returns to the pig pen. An outer cleansing has no effect on the creature's nature and ultimate behavior.

Richard Seymour summarizes what this section says and does not say about these false teachers:

They have 'known the way of righteousness,' which is entirely different than knowing Christ personally. They understand a lot about righteous ways but do not know the Savior. They apply Christian principles to their morality and this helps them in their personal lives [temporarily] but they are not saved. What did they do after knowing and using these principles? They 'turned from them' and are worse off than before...I've been amazed through the years how much religious knowledge skeptics and atheists have who at one time seemed to live by some of God's principles. However, knowledge of God and knowing Him are entirely different...[3]

Commenting on this passage in 2 Peter, Greg Laurie comes to a similar conclusion:

Sometimes we hear about well-known people who claim to have made a commitment to Jesus Christ. Often, it is around election time. When they address Christians, they speak of their great faith in God. After the elections, we seldom hear about it again.

Then there are people who say they are believers, but a month or two later, they go back to their old ways again. They say, "I tried Christianity, but it didn't work for me." But in reality, they never really found Christ.

Others will turn to God when they hit hard times. A while later, you see them going back to their old ways, and you wonder what happened. I would suggest that many of these people never were converted at all. They went through the motions, but Jesus Christ never became a part of their lives. Often, they end up worse than before.

When Jesus Christ truly comes into our lives, He takes up residence. And He doesn't just do a basic housecleaning; He does a thorough one. There is real change. But when a house has only been swept, that is, when someone has made only moral changes, he or she is still vulnerable to the Enemy. This is why we must recognize the futility of simply turning over a new leaf or making a few New Year's resolutions. We must realize the problem is deeper than our moral sins. We must get to the heart of the matter and have

Jesus Christ take residence in our lives and change us from the inside out.[4]

So, as we pray and reach out to some who have gotten off track in the Christian race, we do so with an awareness of the warnings of the apostle Peter. If they are backslidden, we seek to encourage and restore them (Gal. 6:1,2). If they have turned way from the gospel, we endeavor to present valid reasons to substantiate our faith in Christ (1 Pet. 3:15). As believers, we can relate to skeptics with a love and hope that is anchored in our personal confidence in God's assured, secure salvation.

[1] Lee Strobel, *The Case for Faith.* Grand Rapids: Zondervan, 2000) 8-23.

[2] Ray C. Stedman, *Adventuring Through the Bible* (Grand Rapids: Discovery House, 1997), 739.

[3] Richard Seymour, *The Gift,* (LaGrange, WY: Integrity press, 2005) 37,38.

[4] Greg Laurie, *True Conversion,* Harvest Daily Devotion for 6/6/2008.

Blessed Reassurance

Chapter 19
Running to Win the Race

In July of 2008, golf fans were almost as shocked as eighteen year old Michelle Wie. She was one stroke off the lead in the State Farm Classic tournament and was playing her best golf of the year. If she had finished in second place, the $155,252.00 purse would be hers. It would also have secured her a place in the LPGA tour the following season. But Ms. Wie forgot a basic rule in professional golf: she failed to sign her score card before leaving the scoring area. (This signature rule is the heart of golf's honor system.) The reporter further observed, "Wie's short career has been colored by controversy, starting with her disqualification from her pro debut at the 2005 Samsung World Championship for taking an improper drop..." The disqualification made the young athlete forfeit sizable rewards.[1]

The apostle Paul was also concerned about the risk of disqualification. Money or popularity were not his goals; his heart's passion was to make the most of his apostolic ministry. The Lord promises His people rewards at the judgment seat of Christ commensurate with their obedience, devotion, and service to the Kingdom (1 Cor. 3:11-15). Although Paul had already been greatly used by God when he wrote 1 Corinthians (about A.D. 56), he still resolved to avoid immorality, heresy, or passivity—anything that would rob his potential for finishing the race in a worthy manner. Did his reference to being "disqualified" refer to the risk of losing his salvation? Some have interpreted 1 Corinthians 9:27 in this way. Let's take a closer look.

Allusions to Greek athletic contests are used in the New Testament to illustrate principles of Christian living. Paul "fought with wild beasts" at Ephesus (1 Cor. 15:32), and "pressed toward the goal" of his upward call (Phil. 3:14). Several of these symbols occur in 1 Corinthians 9:24-27:

> Do you not know that those who run in a race all run, but one receives the prize? Run in such a way that you may obtain it. And everyone who competes for the prize is temperate in all things. Now they do it to obtain a perishable crown, but we for an imperishable crown. Therefore I run thus: not with uncertainty. Thus I fight: not as one who beats the air. but I discipline my body and bring it into subjection, lest, when I have preached to others, I myself should become disqualified.

The Corinthians would recognize this imagery as referring to the Isthmian Games (almost as popular as the original Olympics). The "race" would envision a foot-race, as in 2 Timothy 4:7:

> "I have fought the good fight, I have finished the race, I have kept the faith" (see also Hebrews 12:1).

The race would be held in a stadium 606 feet in length (from the Greek *stadia*).

All true believers are in this race. The finish line is heaven and the prize is the promise of rewards bestowed upon God's people according to their righteous, loving, Holy Spirit-inspired works (2 Cor. 5:10). The prize given to the champion at the Isthmian games was a pine wreath; its value was in what it represented, not in its substance. The Olympic Games presented a wild olive wreath, and the Pythian games used a laurel one.[2] (I wonder how I would have reacted if I could have won the Namean games? They used a parsley wreath...) The apostle readily notes that these prizes are "perishable," whereas the Lord's rewards are imperishable (1 Cor. 9:25).

To be successful in the games required disciplined exercise and skillful preparation. We are told that "everyone who competes for the prize is temperate in all things" (1 Cor. 9:25). The Greek athlete abstained from unhealthy food, wine, and sexual indulgence. Likewise the Christian is to exhibit the Holy Spirit's fruit of temperance (self control). Drugs and alcohol, sensual sin and aimless living sabotage the disciple who seeks to faithfully "run the race."

Notice Paul's focus on Kingdom priorities:

"Therefore I run thus: not with uncertainty. Thus I fight: not as one who beats the air" (1 Cor. 9:26).

(This is an allusion to boxing.) If the boxer doesn't concentrate, he will take blows and miss his opportunities to land some. This determination included Paul's commitment to govern his body's drives so that they would be his servant instead of his master:

"But I discipline my body and bring it into subjection..." (1 Cor. 9:27).

He is not implying that the body is bad because it is physical (dualism), nor that bodily appetites are bad because of being non-spiritual. God's word affirms the food, drink, sex, and other wholesome pleasures of life are gifts of God and should be used according to His design, wisdom, and boundaries (1 Tim. 4:3,4; 6:17; 1 Cor. 7:2-5).

The passage concludes in verse 27 with an indirect warning:

"But I discipline my body...lest, when I have preached to others, I myself should become disqualified."

What concerned the apostle should concern us as well. What did he mean by being disqualified? Was he inferring that a lack of personal discipline could rob him of his eternal salvation? Does his cautionary statement teach insecurity?

As we have sought to do in these exegetical studies, consider again the context. Was Paul teaching about salvation here? Note that his concern for disqualification related to the prize, not to finishing the race. This hero of the faith was concerned about maximizing his ministry; he was not driven by anxiety that the Lord would reject him if he slipped up. His focus here was on rewards, or "crowns." As he noted later,

> "And if anyone competes in athletics, he is not crowned unless he competes according to the rules" (2 Tim. 2:5).[3]

The desire for the "prize" begins this paragraph and is implied in the grammar three additional times before the last phrase. This passion to excel in his ministry was also the pulse of the preceding context:

> "to the weak I became as weak, that I might win the weak. I have become all things to all men, that I might by all means save some" (1 Cor. 9:22).

The born again believer is fully accepted in the Beloved One (his position), yet should also be zealous to live and serve in a way that pleases the Lord (his practice —Eph. 1:6; 2 Cor. 5:9). Olympic athletes are free to focus on their goal to win if they aren't worrying about being dropped from the team. Likewise, the secure believer is challenged to follow Paul's disciplined example to fulfill his potential in Christ and lay the imperishable wreath at the feet of our Redeemer in glory.[4] One of the rewards is promised to believers who have lived in eager anticipation of Christ's return. Paul penned these words to his son in the faith shortly before being martyred:

> I have fought the good fight, I have finished the race, I have kept the faith. Finally, there is laid up for me the crown of righteousness, which the Lord, the righteous Judge, will give to me on that Day, and not to me only but also to all who have loved His appearing. [2 Tim. 3:7,8].

Let us run this Christian race with security, zeal, and hope.

[1] The Associated Press News Service, July 19, 2008

[2] "Games," *International Standard Bible Encyclopedia.*

[3] Several "crowns" are mentioned in the New Testament, including Phil. 4:1; 1 Thess. 2:19; 2 Tim. 4:8; 1 Pet. 5:4; Rev. 3:11

[4] "The four and twenty elders fall down before him that sat on the throne, and worship him that liveth for ever and ever, and cast their crowns before the throne..." (Rev. 4:10).

Chapter 20
Conclusion

I expect that most readers of this book are born again Christians who have struggled with doubts about their salvation, anxiety that they might lose it, or desire to be equipped to help others with these issues. They may know the promises of salvation mentally, but *have felt unsaved* due to rejection or legalism. Others, however, may come to realize that their notion of "eternal security" has given them an empty, misplaced confidence (such as reliance upon a prayer or altar call instead of Christ Himself). The chapters on assurance urge everyone to make their calling and election sure.

The phrase "once saved, always saved" has been used by some to teach a kind of spiritual life insurance that ignores the need for the vital signs of true faith (1 John 1:7; 2:3,4,9,10,15-17; 3:7,10,14; 4:7,17). Maybe "once saved, *really saved*" would be more accurate—if "saved" means being born again. Justification by faith also brings regeneration by the Holy Spirit, and His presence cannot be hidden. Saving faith is a faith that perseveres and manifests the new life in love-inspired good works. The new person in Christ will have an interest in God's Word, an inclination to pray, and a desire for fellowship and worship.

Some have been taught that the Christian life is a probationary period. Salvation may be genuine but not secure; disciples have desperately to hold on to God lest they ultimately miss heaven. Human nature reasons that total pardon and the gift of eternal life should require more on our part than repentance and faith. This concept of merit robs them of assurance and security and replaces it with a conditional view of redemption. "Salvation is secure *if* we meet certain conditions and maintain a level of spiritual victory." An episode of backsliding triggers fear that they have been abandoned by God or have forfeited His redemption. Instead of helping the believer become more faithful, this insecurity undermines his/her confidence and discourages spiritual progress. Instead, it is the *goodness of God* that leads us to repentance (Rom. 2:4).

The question may arise, What about the person who seems to have believed in Christ, attended church, and shown an interest in spiritual things, yet has become complacent, disinterested, and unchurched? Did this person lose his salvation? Based on the studies in part two, we can answer "no." *He did not lose salvation.* Did he only appear to be truly regenerated, but then fell away? Or is he God's child but—for the time being—is backslidden and carnal? Since God looks at the heart, *only He knows* whether the professing believer is temporarily backslidden (with the expectation of divine chastisement), or that he/she was never regenerated in the first place.

If someone who appeared to be a true Christian can end up unsaved, does this make the issue of spiritual security a *matter of semantics?* Just an issue of how the word "saved" is used? Not at all. Biblical doctrine is always foundational to how one lives. Salvation through the finished work of Christ reflects the character and purposes of God. The Lord is gracious and faithful; He is neither arbitrary nor reluctant to save.

On our part, we need to encourage and warn unfruitful "Christians" lest they be hardened by the deceitfulness of sin (Heb. 3:13). If they are excusing their lack of spiritual vital signs, they may need a "wake up call" lest they wind up with those who will say "Lord, Lord" yet will be sent away from Christ at the Great White Throne. *The best remedy for a backslidden brother or sister is grace-*

oriented discipleship and accountability. Living things grow; true believers will respond to the "bread of life" and confirm their living faith with spiritual growth.

To sum up, Lewis Gregory identifies the primary causes of insecurity in the believer: "Insecurity generally indicates that you are either experiencing feelings of *condemnation* or a sense of *separation* [from God]—or both."[1] Part one of this book has shown that the child of God has been justified by faith and is free from condemnation (Rom 5:1; 8:1). Part two has sought to confirm and defend security by examining a variety of disputed passages.

Conviction of sin by the Holy Spirit (not to be confused with condemnation) is healthy; this corrects us as we walk in the light. However, Satan is the accuser. The devil will try to exploit your times of stumbling to make you feel separated from God. Thankfully, the blood of Christ cleanses us from all sin. Rather than being distanced from God, the believer is spiritually united with Christ in His death, burial, resurrection, and ascension! The child of God will always be kept in this vital union with Christ, as the head is connected with the body, and the branch with the vine.[2]

With confidence in God's Word, we can rest on His promises to save and keep us. Whereas our emotions may be as unpredictable as the weather, God's faithfulness is unshakeable. Jerry Hoffman reached this conclusion in the following poem.

> Driven hard before the wind,
> The sea waves crash around.
> The unrelenting storms assail;
> I rest on solid ground.
>
> The lightning fills the sky above,
> The thunder's ominous sound;
> The rain and hail devouring,
> I rest on solid ground.

The tremors of the earth beneath,
May make my path unsound:
But I am safe, unshaken,
I rest on solid ground.

I rest upon the promise
Of Christ my living King;
That He will be there with me,
Whatever life's storms bring.

I rest in full assurance
That God is in control.
My bark is often battered,
But God protects the soul.

So though the raging storms assail
Wherever they are found.
I need not fear the outcome,
For I rest on solid ground.[3]

Choosing to walk by faith instead of by feelings enables you to rest on this solid ground. A biblical view of assurance and security in Christ is foundational to intimate fellowship with God. Your confidence of eternal life celebrates His amazing grace! The Lord's pardon, acceptance, and indwelling presence inspire you to rejoice in the glorious hope of heaven. Your Christian walk finds secure footing on the promises of God and as you move forward with gratitude for God's wonderful salvation.

[1] Lewis Gregory, *Introducing the New You: The Ultimate Makeover*, (Snellville, GA: Source Ministries International, 2005), 190.

[2] To explore the implication of identification with Christ, see Appendix 1: *The Wheel and Line: Guide to Freedom through the Cross*.

[3] Jerry Hoffman, *Solid Ground*, ChristianPoetry.org (used with permission).

Blessed Reassurance

APPENDICES

Appendix 1
The Wheel and Line:
Freedom Through the Cross
by: Charles R. Solomon

Note: In biblical counseling we find that issues inhibiting assurance and security are frequently resolved when struggling believers are illumined to their personal union with Christ. When they reckon true their co-crucifixion, co-resurrection, and co-ascension with Him, they bypass their soulish doubts and fears. The life "hid with Christ in God" provides blessed reassurance.—J.B.W.

As you read this, you may be in the midst of turmoil. Man may have failed you and God may seem too distant to help. You may have grown up not feeling loved in a way that met your needs. You may never have accepted or loved yourself.

The sense of inadequacy a person can feel in coping with life may run the gamut from mild depression to thoughts of suicide. Because of this, your relationships with those you love may be at the breaking point—or may already be broken seem-ingly beyond repair. If you are at the point of mild despair or utter desperation, this message is tailored to your situation.

God loved you enough to send a Person—His Son, the Lord Jesus Christ—to die on the cross for your sins, to raise Him again and to provide through Him all that is necessary for a victorious, abundant life. Today you either trust that His death met God's condition for the free pardon of your sins or you do not. If you do not, this simple message, and the diagrams to illustrate it, could transform your life as you receive His Life—the Life of the Lord Jesus Christ.

It may be that you have trusted Christ for your salvation but now you are a struggling, defeated believer who has yet to find the way to victory in the Christian life. If either of these situations describes your condition, please study the following thoughts with an open Bible and a prayer that God will illuminate these truths for you.

Your Design

The Wheel Diagram depicts man as a three-part being consisting of spirit,soul and body (1 Thess. 5:23). With the body, through the senses, we relate to our surroundings. The soul, or personality, consists of the functions of the mind, will and emotions. The soul enables us to relate to one another. The spirit enables us to transcend our abilities, limitations, and circumstances as we are regenerated or reborn and indwelt by the Holy Spirit.

Wheel Diagram

Note: Part 1 of *Handbook to Happiness and You—A Spiritual Clinic* allows you to work through this material in the context of a personal counseling interview using the book as a counselor.

The spirit is either related to Adam—Satan's family (see Line Diagram [below])—or to Christ, God's family.

We are born into the world as descendants of Adam and partakers of his nature. That means our spirits are dead to God and alive to Satan. We are in the wrong family! Since our lives came from our first father, Adam, and go back in an unbroken chain to him, we were actually in him when he sinned. Thus, we became sinners before we were physically born. This being the case, we are only doing what comes naturally when we commit sins (Rom. 3:23).

Every life that remains in Adam will eventually end in Hell, as shown in the diagram (Rom. 6:23). Even though we may live very good lives, humanly speaking, we are separated from God unless and until we are born into His family by a spiritual rebirth.

Your Needs

The word "salvation" (1) in the Wheel Diagram means we must have a spiritual birth. Only in this way can we leave the life of Adam and be born into the life of Christ, which is an eternal life, as depicted in the Line Diagram (John 3:3). To be born spiritually, we must recognize or confess that we are in the wrong life and therefore born sinners, with the unavoidable result that we have committed sins. Then we must accept Christ into our lives,because he died for our sins.

In being born spiritually, those who receive the Spirit life of Christ into their spirits by faith become one spirit with Him (1 Cor. 6:17). If they are to have victory over temptation and experience the peace of God in their lives, however, they must have assurance of their salvation. Assurance (2) must be based on the absolutes of God's inerrant Word or it will be fleeting at best.

Many who know (with their minds) that they have personally trusted the Lord Jesus Christ still lack genuine assurance because they have never felt saved. Due to emotional conflicts, many of which stem from childhood rejection, a person's feelings (or emotions) are seldom in harmony with the true facts, either as those facts are described in the Bible or as they exist in the physical world. How we feel things to be is likely to differ from how they really are until Christ becomes central in our lives and heals the damaged emotions.

The believer, old or new, must know that he enters into a secure, eternal spiritual relationship with God through the Lord Jesus Christ (John 5:24) and that he can rely upon and enjoy that security (3). Though many believers know they have accepted Christ, few understand and experience the fact that they are accepted in Him. Most have been forced to earn acceptance on a human basis and feel they also must earn God's acceptance (4), though they have already been accepted entirely through their Christ Life (Eph. 1:6). Every believer is accepted, but many never accept their acceptance, or righteousness (2 Cor. 5:21), by faith.

Few, too, are those who make total commitment (5) or total surrender of their lives to the Lord Jesus Christ. This is an irrevocable decision in which we give God our permission to do anything He wishes in us, with us, to us or through us. We give up all our rights.

Frequently, circumstances degenerate into near chaos after we make such a decision, because God honors our request for Him to take complete control of our lives. If He is to take control then we must lose control, and that is a process that seldom gives us joy! The circumstances or persons God uses to bring us to the end of our control of our lives are often not in themselves spiritual. They sometimes inflict undeserved suffering, but it is just such suffering that accomplishes God's purposes in our lives (1 Pet. 2:20-21; Phil. 1:23-30). At the time of the suffering or chastening (Phil. 3:10; Heb.12:11), it seldom seems a cause for rejoicing, but it is the crucible that produces the holiness we long for.

God's purpose for the believer is to conform him to the image of Christ (Rom. 8:29). Such conformity involves suffering. The "all things" of Romans 8:28 which work together for good are rarely seen as good in themselves, except in retrospect.

Your Inner Conflict

The "S" at the center of the wheel [above] represents the self controlled life or "flesh" (KJV). The flesh is in ascendancy in the lives of most believers for their entire Christian experience. It seeks differing forms, depending upon the individual, to get its needs met by some thing or person in either a negative or a positive way. Money, material things, success, fame, sex, power or any of countless other things can drive or motivate a person and become his central focus when he is dominated by the self-life or flesh. Thus the "flesh" is merely the believer's attempt to live the Christian life in his own strength.

The "flesh," therefore, is a very serious problem for the Christian—as serious as idolatry. For when we replace the centrality of Christ with anything—even ourselves whatever we install on the throne of our lives becomes an idol. God must deal firmly with the flesh. And He does, usually by revealing the self-centered life's inability to cope until the believer, finding his situation unbearable, gives up on himself and becomes interested in exchanging the self-life for the Christ-life.

So long as self (flesh) remains in control, the conflicts depicted in the "soul" (personality) part of the Wheel Diagram will continue. They may become worse with age and increasing responsibilities. Occasionally, a psychologically well-adjusted self-life can cope with circumstances for most of a lifetime, but the results are far from fulfilling.

The psychological deficiencies, along with the guilt (both real and imagined), combine to produce varying degrees of frustration in the self-controlled life. The frustration must be dealt with. Some choose to dump it on others in the form of blows—physical or verbal—while some are more fearful of retaliation and suppress their hostility as best they can. Others suppress anger and frustration because they blame themselves for every problem and annoyance they encounter. When hostility and frustration are suppressed, for whatever reason, they will have an impact in the mind or emotions or both. Internalized hostility or anger often results in depression and/or anxiety in the emotions. Some persons can use their minds to implement various distortions or denials of reality. This enables them to escape the necessity of dealing with the real problem, the self-life.

When the psychological conflict drags on without remedy, however, it commonly results in somatic complaints, as illustrated in the diagram. The physical ailments, though real, actually are symptoms of a deeper problem—the self-life. So are the psychological problems depicted in the "soul" area.

Your Deliverance

These psychological and physiological symptoms begin to disappear when one sees how God can deal with the root problem by dethroning the self-life.

The following Line Diagram shows the "life out of death" principle—God's way of disposing of internal conflict. The horizontal line represents eternal life, the life of Christ. By definition, eternal indicates no beginning or end. It exceeds the boundaries of time. Since Christ is God, He has always lived and always will. His life is the same yesterday, today, and forever (Heb. 13:8). As portrayed at the left of the line, Christ "became flesh" (John 1: 14) and lived in a human body for some 33 years. Then, He was crucified, buried and raised from the dead on the third day (1 Cor. 15:3-4). He continues to live today (Heb. 7:25). Note that eternal life is not only a present and future reality for the believer but also involves the eternal past

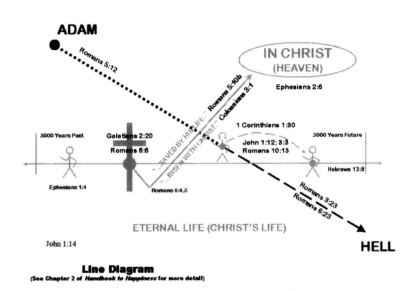

Line Diagram
(See Chapter 2 of *Handbook to Happiness* for more detail)

Until we are born again (John 3:3) we are not in the life of Christ—eternal life—but we are in the spiritually dead life of Adam. One can readily see that if any one of our ancestors, represented by the hatch marks on the diagonal line, had been missing, we also would be missing. Physically speaking, our lives had beginning in Adam, so whatever happened to him also happened to us. When he sinned, we sinned. When he died (spiritually), we died— just as we would have died in our great grandfather if he had died before siring any children. Thus, since spiritual death is separation from God, we were all born dead (spiritually). We need forgiveness for our sins, but we also need life. The Lord Jesus Christ came to give us both—by dying for our sins and by giving us His resurrection life (John 10:10).

If you are a Christian, you already know this much. What you may not yet know is the following; For the believer, physical death is the gateway from life in the world and the presence of sin to life in Heaven and the presence of God. Similarly, another type of death is the gateway from the sinful life of Adam to the eternal life of Christ When a person is "born again," he in the same instant dies. He is born into the life of Christ but he simultaneously dies out of the life of Adam

Christ comes into our lives when we believe in Him and are born again, but that is not all. We are also made "partakers" of His life—eternal life. Romans 6:3 says we are not only baptized into Jesus Christ (His life) but also into His death. We can't occupy two opposite lives at the same time—the life of Adam and the life of Christ

Your Identity

When we receive Christ by faith, it means that His death on the cross counts as payment for our sins. But it means much more. It also means that we enter into a new life—one that extends forever into the past as well as into the future. To put it another way, we exchange our history in Adam—the bad and the good—for an eternal history in Christ. We inherit a new "family tree!" By becoming partakers of Christ's life, we become participants in His death, burial, resurrection, ascension and seating in the heavenlies (Rom. 6:3-6; Gal. 2:20; Eph. 2:6). He only has one life, and this is the life we receive at our new birth (1 John 5:11-12).

Unless and until we know by personal faith experience that we were crucified with Christ, we will continue to try to live for Christ, using the methods we learned in our old self-lives. The conflicts stemming from our history in Adam will go on plaguing and defeating us. But when, by faith, we take our rightful place at the Cross in union with Christ's death and resurrection,then—and only then—can we truly "walk in newness of life" (Rom. 6:4b) where "old things are passed away; behold, all things are become new" (2 Cor.5:17).

The Cross experience (understanding experientially our crucifixion and resurrection with Christ) is the gateway into the Spirit-controlled life (Gal. 5:16). It is life out of death, victory out of defeat—the purpose and answer for suffering in the life of the believer. Our path to the Cross, as well as the Cross itself, is a path of suffering, but it is the only path that leads to the end of suffering.

Are you weary enough of your internal conflict and con-stant defeat to put an end to it by faith? Are you willing to die to all that you are so you can live in all that He is? To do so is to exchange the self-life for the Christ-life and be filled or controlled by the Holy Spirit. To refuse to do so is to continue a walk after the flesh and to grieve the Spirit with a continuation of conflict, suffering and defeat.

Salvation Prayer

If you are tired of the anguish that results from doing things your way, Christ will free you if you will sincerely commit yourself to let Him have His way. If you have never accepted Christ as your personal Savior, your first need is to let God create you anew by giving you spiritual rebirth. You can be born again if you can honestly pray like this:

"Heavenly Father, I have seen that I am a sinner, still in the life of Adam, and that I have committed sins. I believe you sent your only Son, the Lord Jesus Christ, to die in my place for my sins. I also believe He rose again and now lives, and right now I receive Him into my spirit as my Savior. I surrender all that I am, all I have and all I shall be to you. I turn from my sins and my selfish ways to live my new life in Christ. Thank you for saving me. Amen."

Identification Prayer

If you have prayed the "salvation prayer," you have been born again, for God says He gives to all who believe in Christ the privilege of becoming His children (John 1:12). Now, whether you prayed for salvation just now or in the past, praying an "identification prayer" may help you to experience Christ's life of victory and peace. Before this prayer can be effective, you must be truly sick of your self-life; you must be under conviction by the Holy Spirit of trying to live the Christian life in your own strength, and you must be ready to give up control of your life. If this is your condition, pray in this manner.

"Father, thank you for forgiving my sins and taking me out of the life of Adam and grafting me into the life of Christ. Now that I am in Christ, I believe that I was crucified with Him, buried with Him, raised with Him and that I am seated with Him at your right hand. From this moment on, I choose to have your son, Jesus Christ, live His life in me and through me. I consider myself dead to sin and alive to you, and I am counting on the Holy Spirit to make me aware when I forget my death with Christ and try to live His life for Him in my own human wisdom and energy. I choose to yield my total being to you as an instrument of righteousness, allowing no part of me to be used for sin. Thank you for making Christ and his life real to me. Glorify yourself through me. In Jesus' name I pray. Amen."

Appendix 2
The New Venture
by: Reginald Wallace

The New Covenant

True faith gets under the skin and operates in the spirit. It is a heart-covenant, a heart trust, and heart surrender. It touches the very core of your being.

Need it be said that regeneration is not accomplished through the signing of a decision card, or raising the hand in a meeting, or even by going to an "Enquiry room" for personal conversation? Any, or all of these may facilitate the expression or the concession of a quickening faith in the Lord Jesus. Not one of them, however, in and of itself can bring salvation. Heart disease cannot be cured by the external application of a corn plaster. It is Christ, and Christ alone, Who saves. "On Christ the solid Rock I stand." The Irishman's addendum was: "All other rocks are shamrocks." Exactly! The way of life is blessedly simple but it is the only way. Make sure of the validity of your covenant with God. Test your faith by the questions that follow. Be sure of a solid bedrock foundation for your new life, and then go on to live it in the strength of the Lord...

The Very First Thing

What is the acid test of a living faith? If an unwavering YES can be answered to the following questions, there is every reason to rejoice in a God-imparted salvation, and humbly to claim membership in the family of God.

1. Have I recognized that in my natural condition, even up to the noblest attainments of human culture,[1] I am a guilty, undeserving, bankrupt and excuseless sinner,[2] deserving nothing but eternal separation from God, and utterly dependent upon His grace for the gift of Eternal Life?

2. Do I honestly believe in my heart that the Lord Jesus was "made sin"[3] for me, that in His atoning death all the righteous claims of God in respect to my sin were completely and eternally satisfied?

3. Do I believe that God raised Him from the dead,[4] exalted Him to be a Prince and a Saviour,[5] and that He is now "able to save to the uttermost" all who come unto God by Him?[6]

4. Have I trusted Him, by a decisive act of faith and a sincere committal of my whole being to His care, to save me?[7]

5. Do I acknowledge that the only practical evidence of a living faith in Christ as my Saviour is a daily recognition of His Lordship?[8]

6. Am I honestly prepared to confess Christ[9] before men, whenever the Holy Spirit presents an opportunity?

While it is not necessary to understand all the implications of these questions, it is good to examine my own heart in the matter of willingness. The Lord will work it all out in practice if my heart is conquered. Should there be a lurking consciousness that the epoch I called "conversion" involves anything less than these questions imply, then it would be well for me to go to God by way of Calvary, and make sure of a genuine faith. This is always possible. He never refuses the seeking soul. "Other foundation can no man lay than that is laid, which is Jesus Christ."[10]

Am I truly and genuinely "saved"? Do I know that I have passed from death to Life? If there is doubt in my heart, then without any more hesitation, let me turn to God with the prayer: "Lord, save me now."

About Being Quite Sure

It stands to reason that true faith must have a sound basis. It is not credulity or natural speculation, or a mere conjecture of human thinking. Living faith has no less a foundation than the unchanging, inviolate, and inspired truth of God. "Faith cometh by hearing, and hearing by the Word of God."[11] The Scriptures testify of the Lord Jesus.[12] Faith is confidence in a living Person. The Word not only proclaims a complete salvation based upon a perfect atoning sacrifice, but gives the absolute assurance of present and eternal possession.[13] God has spoken the final word and never will He alter what has gone forth from His lips.[14] As I lay aside all questionings and arguments, relying simply upon the written Word of God, so the Holy Spirit witnesses with my spirit that I am a child of God;[15] that is, He makes real to me the effectiveness of the Saviour. Perhaps there is some concern because my "conversion" was not spectacular or sensational or even emotional. Well, God never promised that it would be so. The promise and the process are simplicity itself. God performs a definite miracle of grace the moment a definite condition is fulfilled, that is, acceptance by faith. What about the promise of Revelation 3:20? So far as I knew how, I honestly opened the door of my heart to the Saviour. How do I know He came in? Only by simple reliance on His faithful Word. He said He would. Did He promise feelings, or sensations, or excitement? No! Then why should I look for these? Feelings fluctuate with the weather. God's Word is unchanging.[16]

Remember, however, that a maintained [subjective] assurance depends upon practical obedience to the will of God. If the Holy Spirit is grieved,[17] through self-will or sin, He cannot witness effectively to my salvation because there is contradiction. For this very reason backsliders and carnal believers are often full of doubts. If I walk in the light[18] each day the Spirit's witness will never fail to bring assurance. "It is written..."[19]

Israel was saved by the blood of the slain lamb, but they were to feed on the lamb that they might have strength for the pilgrimage.[20]

[1] Rom. 7:18
[2] Rom. 3:23
[3] 2 Cor. 5:21
[4] Rom. 10:9
[5] Acts 5:31
[6] Heb. 7:25
[7] 2 Tim. 1:12
[8] Rom. 14:9
[9] Luke 12:8
[10] 1 Cor. 3:11
[11] Rom. 10:17
[12] John 5:39
[13] 1 John 5:13
[14] Psalm 89:34
[15] Rom. 8:16
[16] 1 Pet. 1:23
[17] Eph. 4:30
[18] 1 John 1:7
[19] Matt. 4:4
[20] Ex. 12:13, 8

[1] Reginald Wallace, *The New Venture* (Neptune, NJ: Loizeaux Brothers, 1935), 4-9.

Blessed Reassurance

SCRIPTURE INDEX

REFERENCE	PAGE	REFERENCE	PAGE
Jeremiah 31:3	60	Matthew 11:20-24	123
		Matthew 11:28-30	23,28,73
LAMENTATIONS		Matthew 11:29	23
Lam 3:22-24	22.44	Matthew 12:22	88
		Matthew 12:23	88
NAHUM		Matthew 12:24	88
Nahum 1:7	47	Matthew 12:25-28	89
		Matthew 12:31	87
HABAKKUK		Matthew 12:32	87,88
Habakkuk 2:3	102	Matthew 13:25-30	123
Habakkuk 2:4	102	Matthew 19:13	69
		Matthew 19:14	69
ZECHARIAH		Matthew 22:4	79
Zechariah 4:1	76	Matthew 23:37	75
Zechariah 4:2	76	Matthew 25:31-46	90
Zechariah 4:3	77	Matthew 26:39	40
Zechariah 4:4	77		
Zechariah 4:6-10	77	**LUKE**	
		Luke 4:18	89
MATTHEW		Luke 9:23	4
Matthew 4:4	154	Luke 9:57-62	4
Matthew 6:6	53	Luke 10:40-42	19
Matthew 7:13	4	Luke 12:8	154
Matthew 7:14	4	Luke 12:47,48	123
Matthew 7:20	13	Luke 14:17	79
Matthew 7:21-23	12,114	Luke 15:1-31	114
Matthew 7:22	4	Luke 17:6	31
Matthew 7:23	4		

REFERENCE	PAGE	REFERENCE	PAGE
1 Cor 1:30	48	**2 CORINTHIANS**	
1 Cor 1:31	48	2 Cor 2:11	76
1 Cor 2:7	105	2 Cor 3:14-16	106
1 Cor 2:8	105	2 Cor 5:7	28
1 Cor 3:1-3	65	2 Cor 5:9	52,130
1 Cor 3:1-4	67	2 Cor 5:10	14,5212, 128
1 Cor 3:10-15	53		
1 Cor 3:11-15	14,127, 154	2 Cor 5:14	54
		2 Cor 5:15	54
1 Cor 4:16	66	2 Cor 5:17	64,148
1 Cor 6:9	63	2 Cor 5:18-20	75
1 Cor 6:10	63	2 Cor 5:20	53
1 Cor 6:11	64	2 Cor 5:21	47,77, 138,154
1 Cor 6:17	143		
1 Cor 7:2-5	129	2 Cor 10:5	29
1 Cor 9:22	130	2 Cor 13:4,5	5
1 Cor 9:24-27	128	2 Cor 13:5	64
1 Cor 9:25	129		
1 Cor 9:26	112,129	**GALATIANS**	
1 Cor 9:27	112,127, 129	Galatians 1:8	5,108, 117
1 Cor 11:1	66	Galatians 1:9	109
1 Cor 11:29-32	14,51	Galatians 1:13-17	92
1 Cor 12:3	89,101	Galatians 1:17	66
1 Cor 15:2	96	Galatians 1:22	98
1 Cor 15:3-4	147	Galatians 2:16	85,118
1 Cor 15:32	128	Galatians 2:20	20,67, 120,148
		Galatians 3:1-3	19,61, 118

REFERENCE	PAGE	REFERENCE	PAGE
Galatians 3:24	118	Ephesians 2:13	48
Galatians 3:25	118	Ephesians 2:14-22	119
Galatians 3:26-28	107	Ephesians 4:27	76,77
Galatians 5:1	118	Ephesians 4:30	12,56, 63,108, 154
Galatians 5:3	119		
Galatians 5:3-6	117		
Galatians 5:4	119	Ephesians 5:18	14,67
Galatians 5:5	61,119	Ephesians 5:29	53
Galatians 5:6	61,119	Ephesians 6:10-17	15
Galatians 5:13	120	Ephesians 6:12	76
Galatians 5:16	120,148	Ephesians 6:16	76,77
Galatians 5:16-21	67		
Galatians 5:24	65	**PHILIPPIANS**	
Galatians 6:1,2	124	Philippians 1:23-30	144
Galatians 6:7	52	Philippians 2:6-11	40
Galatians 6:15	120	Philippians 3:7-9	90
		Philippians 3:10	144
		Philippians 3:11-14	49
EPHESIANS		Philippians 3:14	112,128
Ephesians 1:3	52	Philippians 3:20	12
Ephesians 1:6	15,130, 144	Philippians 3:21	12
		Philippians 4:1	132
Ephesians 1:12-14	12	Philippians 4:3	53
Ephesians 1:13	35	Philippians 4:13	23
Ephesians 1:23	107		
Ephesians 2:6	148	**COLOSSIANS**	
Ephesians 2:8	5,70,79, 85	Colossians 1:14	53
		Colossians 1:23	96,108, 112
Ephesians 2:9	5,70,85		
Ephesians 2:12	107		

REFERENCE	PAGE	REFERENCE	PAGE
Colossians 1:27	23,66	**2 TIMOTHY**	
Colossians 1:28	95	2 Timothy 1:3	66
Colossians 2:6	20	2 Timothy 1:5	70
Colossians 2:13	48,77,99	2 Timothy 1:12	6,60,71, 154
Colossians 2:14	48,77		
Colossians 2:16,17	119	2 Timothy 2:5	130
Colossians 3:1	7	2 Timothy 2:20-22	54
Colossians 3:3	7	2 Timothy 3:7,8	131
Colossians 3:4	7	2 Timothy 3:15	70
Colossians 3:9	66	2 Timothy 3:16	109,113
Colossians 3:23	4	2 Timothy 3:16,17	45
Colossians 4:12	95	2 Timothy 4:7	113,128
		2 Timothy 4:8	113,132
1 THESSALONIANS		2 Timothy 4:10	112
1 Thess 2:14	98		
1 Thess. 2:19	132	**TITUS**	
1 Thess 5:19	56,63	Titus 1:2	8
1 Thess 5:23	22,142	Titus 2:11	14,79
1 Thess 5:24	22	Titus 2:12	14,79
		Titus 2:13	102
1 TIMOTHY		Titus 2:14	84,102
1 Timothy 1:5	47		
1 Timothy 1:13-17	70	**PHILEMON**	
1 Timothy 2:4	73	Philemon 1:1-25	115
1 Timothy 4:1	108		
1 Timothy 4:3,4	129	**HEBREWS**	
1 Timothy 6:17	129	Hebrews 1:2-4	43
		Hebrews 2:3	94
		Hebrews 2:4	94

REFERENCE	PAGE
JAMES	
James 2:14	4,82
James 2:14-19	4
James 2:14-26	67,81
James 2:15-17	**82**
James 2:18	85
James 2:19	83
James 2:21-23	83
James 2:24	83
James 4:7	77
1 PETER	
1 Peter 1:2	75
1 Peter 1:3-5	41
1 Peter 1:5	112
1 Peter 1:18-20	90
1 Peter 1:23	154
1 Peter 2:9	48
1 Peter 2:10	48
1 Peter 2:11	65
1 Peter 2:20,21	144
1 Peter 3:7	56
1 Peter 3:15	124
1 Peter 5:4	132
2 PETER	
2 Peter 1:3	5
2 Peter 1:4	5,64

REFERENCE	PAGE
2 Peter 1:10	5,72
2 Peter 2:17	123
2 Peter 2:20-22	95,122, 123
2 Peter 3:9	73
2 Peter 3:18	14,71
1, 2, 3 JOHN	
1 John 1:7	48,133, 154
1 John 1:7-9	14
1 John 1:9	49
1 John 2:1	34,74, 76
1 John 2:2	34,74, 110,122
1 John 2:3,4,9,10	133
1 John 2:19	5
1 John 3:7,10,14	133
1 John 3:20	60
1 John 3:21	60
1 John 4:7-16	4
1 John 4:19	14
1 John 5:3	63
1 John 5:4	112
1 John 5:5	112
1 John 5:9	8
1 John 5:11,12	148
1 John 5:13	154

PUBLICATIONS FROM GRACE FELLOWSHIP INTERNATIONAL

 Handbook to Happiness, by Charles R. Solomon $ 10.95

 The Ins and Out of Rejection, by Charles R. Solomon $ 10.95

 The Rejection Syndrome and the Way to Acceptance, by Charles R. Solomon $ 10.95

 Handbook to Happiness & You, by Charles R. Solomon $ 10.95

 Handbook for Christ-Centered Counseling, by Charles R. Solomon $ 10.95

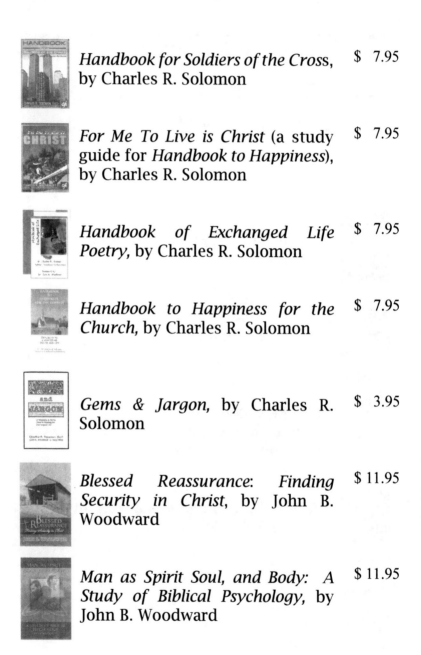

Handbook for Soldiers of the Cross, by Charles R. Solomon $ 7.95

For Me To Live is Christ (a study guide for *Handbook to Happiness*), by Charles R. Solomon $ 7.95

Handbook of Exchanged Life Poetry, by Charles R. Solomon $ 7.95

Handbook to Happiness for the Church, by Charles R. Solomon $ 7.95

Gems & Jargon, by Charles R. Solomon $ 3.95

Blessed Reassurance: Finding Security in Christ, by John B. Woodward $ 11.95

Man as Spirit Soul, and Body: A Study of Biblical Psychology, by John B. Woodward $ 11.95

$ 7.95

The New Life, by Reginald Wallace

$ 4.95

How to Exchange Your Life for a New One, by Phil Jones

$ 11.95

Grace Discipleship Course, by Lee Turner

$ 11.95

Advanced Grace Discipleship Course, by Lee Turner

To receive the author's weekly GraceNotes email Bible study, subscribe at www.gracenotebook.com.

For additional materials, visit our websites:

www.GraceFellowshipIntl.com
www.SolomonPublications.org
www.GFICounselingInstitute.org

Blessed Reassurance

CPSIA information can be obtained at www.ICGtesting.com
Printed in the USA
LVOW09s0811020215

425312LV00001B/2/P